Exercise
of Authority:

Surveyor Thomas Owen
and the paving, cleansing and
lighting of Georgian Dublin

An act of Parliament passed in the year 1774 ... for new-paving the streets ... has contributed greatly to the beauty and convenience, as well as healthiness of the city.

Pool & Cash, *Views of the most remarkable public buildings, monuments and other edifices in the city of Dublin* (Dublin, 1780), p. 16.

Our miserable streets, the curse of their inhabitants, the laugh, the scorn of foreigners ...

Anon., *Observations on the paving acts* (Dublin, 1782), p. 3.

Cover Images:

Saint Catherine's, Thomas Street, Dublin by James Malton (1792). Ink and watercolour (53.3 x 77.4cm) (NGI 2186; photograph courtesy of the National Gallery of Ireland ©).

Section of text from Dublin Paving Board minute book, vol. 6 (DCA/PB/Mins6, 1779) (courtesy of Dublin City Library and Archives).

Exercise of Authority:

Surveyor Thomas Owen and
the paving, cleansing
and lighting of Georgian Dublin

Finnian Ó Cionnaith

Dublin
Dublin City Council
2015

First published 2015 by
Dublin City Council

www.dublincommemorates.ie

Text © the contributors 2015
Concept © Dublin City Public Libraries and Archives
Designed by: Yellowstone Communications Design
Printed by: Johnswood Press

ISBN: 978-1-907002-23-6 (Hardback)
         978-1-907002-30-4 (Paperback)

Distributed by
Four Courts Press
Malpas Street
Dublin 7
www.fourcourtspress.ie

Contents

Acknowledgements

I would very much like to thank the individuals and institutions that I have encountered over the course of researching this book that have assisted and helped in a wide variety of ways. Firstly I am honoured to have this publication included in Dublin City Council's History of Dublin Engineering series. As such I would like to thank Michael Philips, Dublin City Engineer, for his generous support and Dr Mary Clark, City Archivist, for her advice, guidance and encouragement. It is a privilege to bring the works of the Dublin Paving Board to light as part of such a wonderful series on the history of engineering in the city.

I would also like to thank Michael Ann Bevivino for her very welcome input and assistance in the editing process. Others who I would like to mention include the staff of the Dublin City Library and Archive, as well as those of the National Library of Ireland, Thomas Curran of the Survey and Mapping Division (Dublin City Council), Maria O'Shea of Marsh's Library, the team at Yellowstone Design, Dr Jacinta Prunty (Maynooth University) for initially introducing me to the works of the Dublin Paving Board, Prof. Marian Lyons and Dr Michael Potterton (Maynooth University), Anthony Tierney and the staff of Four Courts Press, Paul Ferguson (Trinity College Dublin), Colum Ó Riordan (Irish Architectural Archive) and my supportive family, Philomena and Fiachra.

This book is the story of a city, an institution and an individual. It is unlikely that Thomas Owen ever thought that his work would be investigated as it has been for this study; however, I would still like to thank him and his employers at the Dublin Paving Board for leaving such an interesting, detailed and occasionally controversial legacy for modern researchers to explore.

For Donna

Abbreviations

DCA   Dublin City Archives

DMP   Dublin Metropolitan Police

IAA   Irish Architectural Archive

ML   Marsh's Library

PB/Mins Dublin Paving Board Minute Books, vols 1–36 (1774–1801), DCA

PWC   Pipe Water Committee

WSC   Wide Streets Commission

Illustrations

Preface

Mary Clark, Dublin City Archivist

From the 1770s to the mid-nineteenth century the commissioners for paving the streets of Dublin, commonly known as the Paving Board, were responsible for the paving, lighting and cleansing of the capital. This important municipal body played a significant role in the development of Georgian Dublin and left behind a rich archival legacy in the form of a large collection of manuscript minute books. These records, currently held by the Dublin City Library & Archive, provide meticulous documentary evidence of the workings of a vital urban service provider while offering insight into the complex urban world that constituted the city during this period.

Prior to its foundation, the maintenance of Dublin's streets was a haphazard affair with the city's patchwork of diverse and divergent parishes bearing responsibility for services within their borders. The Paving Board took this misbalanced system and placed the city under one hierarchical organisation capable, in theory, of helping the rapidly growing city cope with the changes it encountered.

The legacy of the Paving Board can still be seen today in the setts and granite curbstones which can be found in Dublin's historic core and yet this book, being the first history of this important body, looks far beyond the physical evidence left behind by this organisation. May I congratulate the author, Finnian O'Cionnaith, for developing this new insight into Dublin and this history of its infrastructure.

Exercise of Authority is the second in a new series of books issued by Dublin City Council to explore the engineering history and heritage of the city. This richly-illustrated book is essential for a complete understanding of Georgian Dublin.

Foreword

Michael Phillips, former Dublin City Engineer

The provision of public services is one of the paramount duties of any local government. Without addressing the development, maintenance and repair of a city, its growth and prosperity will inevitably be greatly restricted to the detriment of its citizens. The founding of the Dublin Paving Board in 1774 stands as an important milestone in Dublin's urban infrastructural history at a time when the modern city that we know today was taking shape. Without paving, cleansing and lighting services late eighteenth-century Dublin would have struggled to become one of the city's finest eras so frequently mentioned as its 'golden age'.

One of the primary strengths of this publication is its examination of not only the work of the Paving Board on the streets of the city, but also its complex, and frequently altered organisational hierarchy. By focusing on the initial years of the Paving Board in this book, O'Cionnaith explores both the mechanics of establishing a vital department of city management and the social and political world which heavily influenced its work. Of particular note is the tension between local and national government for control of the board exposing significantly wider issues affecting Irish society at the time. By choosing surveyor Thomas Owen as this book's central character, O'Cionnaith adds a vital human element and focuses on the importance of those who were present to witness such events yet who are often overlooked by history. Owen's practical skill and central role with the board directly links his story with that of the development of Dublin. Despite his occasionally chequered career he provided witness to the internal workings of an organisation that was often kept behind closed doors.

Such bodies are very much products of their times and it is through the exploration of the Paving Board's success and failures that we, the reader, gain new awareness into the wider world of eighteenth-century Dublin. This volume is a welcome addition to the history of Dublin engineering series which is being published by Dublin City Council and may I commend the author, Finnian O'Cionnaith, on his initiative in bringing us new insight into Georgian Dublin.

Introduction

Life in a city can be said to be shared between its buildings and its streets. The buildings, providing homes, work and shelter, are often the primary focus of our metropolitan attention, yet the streets, that visible, public arterial network, are where the majority of any population engages with its surrounding environment. They are a communal forum which we share with countless strangers on a daily basis and our temporary presence in such a medium allows each of us to contribute to the character of our urban areas. Streets keep a city alive. This book examines a brief period in Dublin's history where the state of the city's streets, and how they were managed, was radically altered by a small group of men with immense power over the populace. The Dublin Paving Board, founded in 1774, applied a systematic approach to the paving, cleansing, and later lighting, of a city whose dilapidated civic infrastructure was struggling with rapid urban expansion.

What was the Paving Board? One word: authority. Its power over the street life of the city, from maintaining footpaths and roads, to controlling Dublin's turbulent markets and residential areas, gave this body vast control over the residents of the city. It attempted to stamp a form of Georgian conformity on an environment in the painful process of transforming from a late medieval port to the second capital of a global empire. The Paving Board, created by an act of parliament and made up of powerful politicians and civic representatives, was a solution to bringing Dublin's various urban street problems together under one central authority and, like its larger and more glamorous contemporary cousin the Wide Streets Commission (WSC), attempted to apply a logical approach to help the city cope with its evolution. Many of the issues encountered by the board could be considered strangely familiar to modern Dubliners – unending road works, hostility towards taxation in an era of austerity, concerns over street crime, protests over privatisation of public services, problems with waste collection and even repeated attempts to manage traffic passing through College Green. The board's was a Sisyphean task. Any urban environment is under constant change and the board struggled throughout its lifetime with insufficient income, corrupt employees and repeated (and often unwelcome) parliamentary intrusions into its methods.

Dublin in the late eighteenth-century was undergoing substantial changes physically, politically and socially, that would bring it from the confusion and strife of the previous centuries towards a model more familiar to us today. The conflicts that had ravaged the country in the seventeenth century were over and the country would remain relatively peaceful until the 1798 rebellion. Despite the peace, Ireland was not immune from hardship, with a devastating famine sweeping the island in 1741, followed by an exponential population growth in the following decades. Dublin was not exempt from this growth and the city's population roughly trebled to approximately 180,000 during this period.[1] The city, home of the Irish Parliament and a major commercial port not only for the country but for the wider empire, was a bustling metropolis whose centuries-old infrastructure strained under its growing requirements. Coffee houses, bookshops, taverns, apothecaries, butchers, markets and stalls lined the streets where servants, artisans, gentry and the penniless fought for space among the passing carts and carriages. The core of Dublin was a warren of narrow medieval streets, some of which were paved, others simply compacted earth not designed for the level of traffic that they were forced to take. Footpaths for pedestrians were often non-existent. Drains struggled to cope with the mounting waste from such a tightly packed community while many streets degraded to such an extent that they were impassable during periods of poor weather. Filth was everywhere as were the diseases and vermin associated with it. At night, poor lighting provided Dublin's criminal elements with the perfect setting to prey on their victims while the city's diverse parish authorities struggled to find a uniform method of improving street life across the city.

Dublin was still heavily affected by the turbulent wars, religious and political upheaval of the seventeenth century. Despite partially successful attempts at retraction, the city's sizeable Catholic minority was still officially excluded from public office under the Penal Laws, yet Catholic merchants thrived on the volume of trade that the city's docks brought in. By the late eighteenth century the city walls required to keep the populace safe during the 1641 rebellion, Cromwell's Irish campaign (1649–53) and the Williamite Wars (1689–91), were in the process of being slowly removed, highlighting the calmer socio-political environment that existed prior to the 1798 rebellion. The Irish Parliament on College Green, though roughly put in its place as subservient to Westminster by the Declaratory Act (1720),[2] was still the central focus of the country's political world and would be the arena where many of the battles concerning the Paving Board would be fought, both literally and figuratively. While parliament may have been the core of the city's focus, its peripheries were equally important. The rapidly developing new neighbourhoods emerging around the now iconic Georgian squares, mostly to the city's eastern side, were firmly in the hands of private ownership, resulting in a mismatched level of progress across Dublin. The south-west of the city was the focus of industry, primarily in linen and woollen weaving around the Liberties and the Coombe, in addition to home to large populations of poor and destitute Dubliners. The north-west, apart from the large army barracks in Oxmanstown, was still relatively underdeveloped in comparison to the dense medieval city

---

1   Ian McBride, *Eighteenth-century Ireland* (Dublin, 2009), p. 108.
2   6. Geo. I, c. 5. [Ire.] (1758).

centre. Though significantly smaller than modern Dublin, the city was still a large metropolitan centre by late eighteenth-century European terms and the largest urban area in Ireland.

The Paving Board was not the only organisation working towards the improvement of the city during this era and it should be seen in context as just one of a number of institutes working towards civic modernisation. The WSC, a more powerful and significantly wealthier contemporary to the Paving Board, had been created in the 1750s to replace Dublin's maze of narrow streets with modern, well-planned and wider thoroughfares and allow greater ease of movement. This body was responsible for the construction of many of Dublin's most important thoroughfares including Parliament Street (1750s), North Frederick Street and the continuation of Sackville Mall to the River Liffey (1780s) and D'Olier and Westmoreland Streets (1800s).[3] Such significant changes to the city were also aided by the Ballast Board, responsible for developing Dublin's port, the building of both the Royal and Grand Canals by their respective development companies and the Pipe Water Committee (PWC), who, in the process of providing Dublin's homes with access to water, caused innumerable problems for the Paving Board. Despite each organisation working towards the betterment of the city, they were independent and separate bodies responsible for their own finances, plans and building work, with only nominal control from either Dublin Corporation or the Irish Parliament. Though each represented a significant step away from previous attempts at urban development, their independence led to a lack of an overall coherent plan resulting in an often disjointed, confused and at times conflicting level of progress across the city. Among this array of organisations, the Paving Board was perhaps the only one to operate on every single street in the city, impacting the lives of the entire populous.

At the heart of the board's operations was surveyor Thomas Owen. Owen was a minor character in Dublin's overall history; it is through his story, however, that we can explore a much wider range of events. Owen may perhaps seem like an unusual and obscure character for this story given the many well-documented personalities also involved with the board during this time, but there are a number of criteria that single him out as an individual of great importance during the Paving Board's formative years. Firstly, he was a senior technical officer to the board who began his work in its earliest days, and who was present for many of the most important decisions that they made. These decisions were often greatly influenced by his measurements. This allows not only the early years of the organisation's labour to

---

3   Finnian Ó Cionnaith, *Mapping, measurement and metropolis: how land surveyors shaped eighteenth-century Dublin* (Dublin, 2012), pp 187–209.

be reviewed but also exposes the often turbulent internal workings of a complex and at times controversial body. Aside from his attendance in the boardroom, Owen was present for many of the board's external interactions with the citizens of late eighteenth-century Dublin. He was the Paving Board's witness to events on the ground, where the board of commissioners was rarely seen in an official capacity, guiding them through the multifaceted and at times overwhelming duty of improving mile upon mile of Dublin's streets. He regularly acted a human buffer between the commissioners, their contractors and the ordinary citizens of Dublin, and provides the modern reader with detailed insight to street life during that era. Thirdly, and perhaps what separates him most from his colleagues, was his work as a surveyor. Spatial measurement (area, volume, length, etc.) were key to such work as without it the board members were unable to quantify their task at hand. Without his work the organisation's financial planning, though never praiseworthy, would have collapsed under the weight of the city's needs. His measurements allowed the Paving Board to make well-informed decisions, assign adequate funding and monitor its progress one square yard at a time. As such, his effort was a key factor in both the daily and long-term strategic work of the organisation and a vital aspect of its successes. Though a highly capable individual, Owen was no hero. Throughout his career with the Paving Board, he was subject of a series of complaints relating to poor work practices and questions over his honesty. Yet within that organisation he was not alone in coming under criticism.

This book focuses on the tumultuous years 1774–87. This era marked the foundation of the Paving Board, its administrative set-up and initial projects, and covers the length of time that Thomas Owen worked for the organisation. Throughout this short period the Paving Board underwent a series of massive internal changes as a result of several damning reports and scandals into alleged corruption and financial irregularities. These revelations brought Dublin Corporation and the Irish Parliament into repeated conflict, with the board being the inadvertent cause of a street riot that resulted in the Irish House of Commons being invaded by angry protestors, followed by attempts to greatly curtail the power of free speech of the press. These dramatic events subsequently led to control of Dublin's streets being slowly wrestled away from the corporation and power being passed to a small unelected cadre who had the authority to fine, or even imprison (outside of the normal criminal justice system of the era), any Dublin resident who disobeyed their rules.

The structure of this book follows the successes and failures of the first three incarnations of the Dublin Paving Board in detail, with a shorter discussion on the fourth and fifth boards that existed during the nineteenth century. It examines the circumstances that led to the board's foundation, its duties and finances, as well as its attempts to enforce rules on Dublin's citizens. The conditions of each collapse and restoration of the Paving Board during this time and the repeated efforts to reform the body are examined in individual chapters. These are intertwined by stories and examples of its work on the streets, a look at the vicious cycle of financial short falls and increasing workload that it was caught in and its often raw relationships with the Irish Parliament, Dublin Corporation, the city's parishes and the capital's residents. This book aims to tell the combined history of a board entrusted with improving the second city of the British Empire, the daily lives and concerns of Georgian Dubliners and the importance of spatial measurement in late eighteenth-century civil engineering works.

Much of the information used within comes from the handwritten and highly detailed minute books the board kept from its foundation. Each three-hundred- to four-hundred-page minute book, covering approximately a year in the life of the Paving Board, exposes the inner workings of a complex organisation, its communications with the citizens of Dublin and the problems it encountered during the course of its duties. These records offer unparalleled first-hand insight into how this body went about its daily business and the manner in which it dealt with the multitude of problems that it encountered. Included throughout the book are multiple anecdotes of the Paving Board's work on the streets of eighteenth-century Dublin and its interactions with the city's inhabitants. These stories range from the mundane to the bizarre and, apart from providing the vital human element to which we can all relate, also highlight the ever-changing environment and complexities that Dublin presented during this era. The daily work of the board was interspersed with violence, theft, protest, strikes and seemingly endless complaints.

Through their 'energetic exercise of authority'[4] the Dublin Paving Board sought control over the thoroughfares that made up the city and, in the process, affected the lives of all Dubliners whether rich or poor, noble or destitute.

---

4   John LaTouche, et al., *Report of the commissioners appointed to enquire into the conduct and management of the corporation for paving, cleansing and lighting the streets of Dublin* (Dublin, 1806), p. 29.

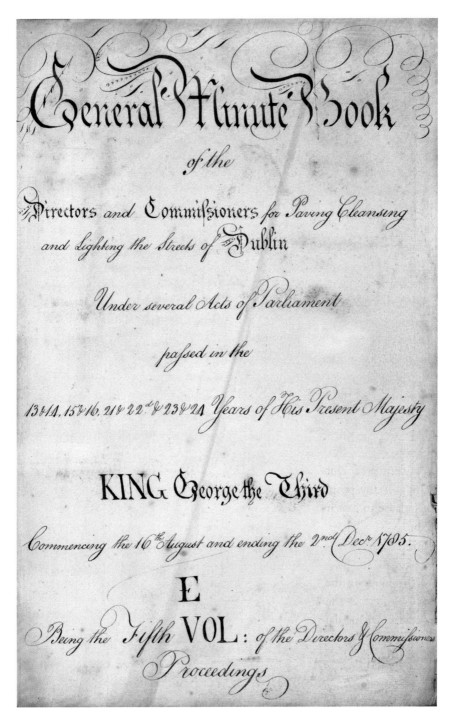

General Minute Book

of the

Directors and Commissioners for Paving Cleansing
and Lighting the Streets of Dublin

Under several Acts of Parliament

passed in the

13 & 14, 15 & 16, 21 & 22.nd & 23 & 24 Years of His Present Majesty

KING George the Third

Commencing the 16th August and ending the 2nd Decr 1785.

E

Being the Fifth VOL: of the Directors & Commissioners
Proceedings

0.0   Title page of a Dublin Paving Board minute book. (DCA/PB/Mins16, 16 Aug.–2
Dec. 1785) (courtesy of Dublin City Library and Archives).

1 The origins of the Dublin Paving Board (1774)

The commissioners for paving the streets of Dublin, also commonly known as the Dublin Paving Board, was founded at a meeting in early June 1774 at the Navigation Board House in the centre of Dublin. Present at the inaugural meeting were seventeen members of city's political and civil hierarchy.[5] This initial meeting simply established the body's existence with no real decisions reached or agreed upon, yet it marked the beginning of a series of radical changes that would affect the day-to-day lives, and pockets, of the city's residents for decades to come.

This body had been invested with authority by an act of the Irish Parliament[6] to enforce, tax and regulate rules to remove public nuisances from Dublin's streets (namely projecting buildings, sheds, signs and stalls), organise and monitor the disposal of street waste by teams of waste removal crews known as 'scavengers', pave the city's thoroughfares, maintain the sewers and eventually run fountain maintenance and street lighting throughout the city.[7] It was hoped that the Paving Board would 'tend greatly to the free intercourse, health, and safety of the said streets'[8] and bring an increased level of order to Dublin's bustling streets. To sponsor this organisation each resident was to pay a tax rate proportional to the value of their property, collected by the board and used as a centralised fund to finance its work across the city.[9] Enforcement of this often unpopular tax was aided by the board's power to summon individuals who violated their directives or refused to cooperate and level substantial fines and/or prison sentences independent of the usual criminal justice system. One commentator at the time expressed his bewilderment at Dublin Corporation for not protesting such extraordinary powers, stating 'Many people think our city members were asleep when they suffered that clause to pass in the Paving Act, which subjects a poor man to two months imprisonment, if he either refuses, or is unable to pay his quota'.[10] Despite their initial drive, the Paving Board was not the first organisation to try and regulate the paving, cleansing and lighting of the city, nor were the street conditions in the 1770s unique to the city's history. Attempts at regulating Dublin's streets were almost as old as the city itself. One of the first recorded ordnances specifically related to paving dates back to 1336 when King Edward III granted permission

---

5   Including Lord Ranelagh (d. 1797), David LaTouche Jr. (1729–1817), Luke Gardiner (1745–98), Dr William Clement (d. 1782), Andrew Caldwell (1733–1808); 6 June 1774 (PB/Mins/1, p. 1).
6   15 & 16 Geo. III, c. 20 [Ire.] (1775).
7   14 Sept. 1784 (PB/Mins/13, p. 2).
8   15 & 16 Geo. III, c. 20 [Ire.] (1775).
9   27 Oct. 1779 (PB/Mins/6, p. 246).
10   *Leinster Journal*, 11 June 1774.

for Dublin's streets to be surfaced.[11] Organisation of street maintenance evolved sporadically between then and the eighteenth century, with the Paving Board being the final product of a number of similar attempts at applying authority to the often chaotic thoroughfares.

Dublin's parishes were responsible for many of these duties prior to the establishment of the Paving Board. For most of the city's residents their local parish authorities, rather than the central Irish Parliament or even Dublin Corporation, had the greatest impact on their lives. Each parish was responsible for most of the services within their borders, including street maintenance, and would have been the visible and daily exposure that most Dubliners had to local government. Despite Dublin Corporation bearing overall responsibility for the city, parishes played a very important part in civic administration dating back to the medieval period. These ancient administrative bodies were still of such importance by the eighteenth century that their complex and winding borders were included as a primary form of municipal boundary for Charles Brookings' 1728 city survey.[12]

An act passed by the Irish Parliament in 1717[13] was one of the first attempts in the eighteenth century to apply order to the administration of the city's streets across Dublin's diverse parishes through a centralised body formed by the lord mayor, a city sheriff and two aldermen. This small group, in conjunction with parochial committees, was assigned many of the directives granted to the Paving Board later in the century including paving, waste removal and street lighting.[14] The 1717 act, although significantly smaller and less detailed than the act that created the Paving Board, highlighted many of the primary problems that plagued the streets of Dublin at the time:

> Whereas the public pavements in the city and suburbs of the city of Dublin ... are in many places of the said city very much out of repair, and in several places raised to such a height ... that carriages, coaches, or horses, cannot with safety pass over the same: and whereas many encroachments are made on the streets ... to the great dangers of the inhabitants: and great quantities of coal-ashes, and other filth of late have been and are daily thrown into the streets.[15]

---

11   John Warburton, *History of the city of Dublin* (London, 1818), p. 384.
12   Charles Brooking, *A map of the city and suburbs of Dublin* (London, 1728).
13   4 Geo. I, c. 2 [Ire.] (1717).
14   This act was amended in 1719 to bring in the use of grand juries to assist with financial estimates and valuations (6 Geo. I, c. 15 [Ire.] (1719).).
15   4 Geo. I, c. 2 [Ire.] (1717).

Removing building nuisances and fencing unoccupied lots were also issues to which the lord mayor and his team had to apply their consideration. However, particular attention in the 1717 act was focused on the city's dangerous traffic due to a high number of pedestrian fatalities

> through the negligence of carts, dray-men and car-men, riding [through] the streets of Dublin ... aged and other persons and children are frequently maimed, wounded and killed: for preventing such mischiefs for the future ... any cart, dray, or car ... [shall have] some other person or persons on foot to guide or conduct the same.[16]

Violation of these traffic safety rules would result in fines starting at ten shillings, imprisonment or, for the most serious wrongdoings, offenders would be 'publickly whipt through the streets of Dublin'.[17]

By the 1720s, authority over city's street life had shifted from the lord mayor back to the parishes. A detailed agreement was drawn up between the lord mayor and the churchwardens of Dublin in 1725, and later added to by an act of parliament,[18] on how the city's infrastructure was to be maintained and provides great insight into the day-to-day activities that would affect each household in Dublin.[19] The primary importance of this agreement was its effort to enforce a form of standardisation across a city where individual parishes, with often widely diverging levels of income from taxation, had extensive powers as local administrative areas. Conformity was the goal. Another important aspect of the 1725 agreement tackled waste management. Scavengers where hired to remove waste every two days from the city, suburbs and liberties 'upon pain to forfeit five shillings for every default' and it was the responsibility of each household to have their waste presented for collection by the scavengers and the front of their house swept by 9am. Late presentation of waste by households resulted in a fine of one shilling, split between the informer who reported the offence and the poor of the parish. Each parish was required to appoint two churchwardens to act as local inspectors to enforce these rules and for the 'care of society and accommodation of our neighbours'. This attempt at developing a harmonious community effort, however, was not ideal. With each parish charging their residents for services, the gap between the wealthier and poorer parts of the city meant that a uniform standard across

---

16   Ibid.
17   Ibid, clause xi.
18   3 Geo. II, c. 13 [Ire.] (1725).
19   Dublin church wardens agreement concerning the lighting and cleaning of streets (ML, 1725).

Dublin was difficult, if not impossible, to achieve. Even with the more focused authority that the Paving Board would bring in the 1770s, financial revenue from poor portions of the city could often lead to significant problems, as was lamented by the later commissioners:

> the debt of the late seventh division is a great weight on this corporation ... and [causes] the difficulty of collecting the tax in the liberty of Donore (which is principally inhabited by poor manufacturers).[20]

Despite the issues that financial income would play, the eventual centralisation of street maintenance was a positive step in achieving a consistent standard across the city. The foundation of the Dublin Paving Board was also no doubt influenced by events in London with the passing of the Westminster Paving Act (1762), where a single body was created to systematically organise the paving, cleansing and lighting of the city, replacing an archaic system similar to the Dublin parish model.[21] The Westminster act appointed individual commissioners to be responsible for sections of the city while organising their work as a unified, hierarchal body, thus being able to pool resources and ensuring, in theory, that the sections of the city in most need of infrastructural repair were given priority, rather than those who could most easily afford it. It also meant that paving, in particular, would be laid down and maintained as uniformly as possible, giving in to that Georgian-era ideal of urban conventionality: '[The Westminster Paving Act led to] all those improvements which have contributed to make London, as far as comfort and convenience are concerned, the finest ... city in the world'.[22] Where London led, Dublin followed. 'An act for paving the streets, lanes, quays, bridges, squares, courts and alleys' of Dublin was passed by the lord lieutenant, Earl Simon Harcourt (1714–77), on 4 June 1774, with the initial meeting of the Paving Board taking place two days later.[23] This board was the product of the Irish Parliament rather than the local authority, Dublin Corporation, and so despite the corporation being responsible for daily management and strategy, and with many of the commissioners being members of the corporation, the board was ultimately answerable to parliament.[24] This staggered administrative arrangement would be a source of tension between the two bodies in the years to come.

---

20   28 Oct. 1782 (PB/Mins/10, p. 96).
21   Linda Frock, *Building capitalism* (London, 1991), p. 116.
22   *The Penny Magazine*, 18 Mar. 1837.
23   *Leinster Journal*, 5 June 1774.
24   Another example of this related to the improvement of Dublin was the Wide Streets Commission, created under an act of the Irish parliament (31 Geo. II, c.19 [Ire.] (1757)).

As stated, the first meeting of the Paving Board was held simply to confirm that the body existed; however its second meeting, attended by thirty-nine city representatives and presided over by the lord mayor, set to work on organising the board into a functional organisation.[25] Dublin Corporation at the time was divided into two houses: the common (lower) house to which freemen of the city could be elected by their respective guilds and the aldermen (upper) board consisting of twenty-four members. Aldermen were elected for life, unless the holder chose to resign or converted to Catholicism, and the lord mayor was annually elected by them from among their number.[26]

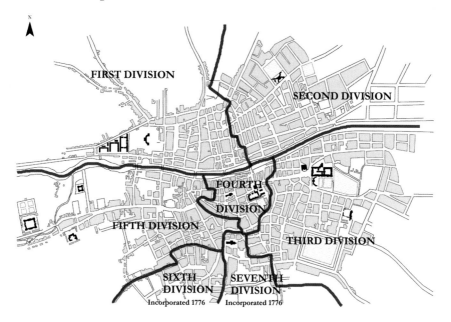

1.1   Dublin c.1774 with the administrative divisions set up by the Dublin Paving Board across the city (map by author).

At the second sitting of the Paving Board, the city was divided into five administrative divisions (Fig. 1.1), each consisting of a number of parishes, and an organisational chain of command was established (see appendix).[27] Three aldermen and three common council members were elected from among the members of Dublin Corporation to represent each division respectively, with each parish within a division being represented by a parochial committee consisting of between one and five members. Parochial committees were elected by Protestant parishioners

25   8 June 1774 (PB/Mins/1, p. 2).
26   Ruth McManus and Lisa Marie Griffith (eds), *Leaders of the city* (Dublin, 2013), p. 21.
27   Div. 1: St Michan's, St Paul's; Div. 2: St Thomas', St Mary's; Div. 3: St Anne's, St Peter's; Div. 4: St Michael's, St Werburgh's, St Nicholas Within; Div. 5: St Nicholas Without, St Catherine's, St James'; 8 June 1774 (PB/Mins/1, p. 2).

only. Each division was represented on the main board by a commissioner[28] who, with the assistance of the elected aldermen and common council members, was empowered to raise funds through taxation and to legally enforce the decisions of the board. A quorum of seven was required at board level in order to pass resolutions.[29] Each parochial committee in Dublin was required to bring reports of streets in need of repair to their respective divisional committee, who would then pass these to the commissioners. For its seal the board chose an image of a harp over a pickaxe with the words 'Corporation for paving the city of Dublin'.[30]

With the Paving Board's administrative control established, the board set about filling positions for officers to allow it to carry out its work. Each officer was to play a key role in the day-to-day duties of the Paving Board and their performance would reflect directly on the ability of the overall establishment. The commissioners' officers were re-elected each year unless the board found reasons not to have them return or found a more qualified or suitable replacement.[31] John Finlay was elected as the board's first treasurer on a voluntary basis as a resolution had already been passed 'that there shall not be any salary allowed for executing [this] office'.[32] Richard Bragg won an election held at the Tholsel to be the first clerk of the Paving Board, in competition against a Mr Dalton and a Revd Murray. This was a salaried position, initially advertised at £30 but that was then increased to £40 'after some debate'.[33] The clerk was responsible for managing the extensive communications the Paving Board undertook in addition to documenting their meetings and issuing summonses to citizens of Dublin. These summonses were mostly due to reports from the inspectors of nuisances, who were the Paving Board's direct link to the streets and citizens of the city in each division. The inspectors were required to

> perambulate their respective divisions, & view the quay walls that are fallen or decayed ... the several nuisances & obstructions in the markets ... set out windows, show boards or other projections erected without license of this corporation, and nuisances in general on the footways or carriages.[34]

---

28 James Agar (1734–89), Sydenham Singleton (d. 1800), Major Charles Vallancey (1726–1812), Travers Hartley and Nicholas Mornington; 29 June 1774 (PB/Mins/1, p. 10).
29 15 & 16 Geo. III, c. 20 [Ire.] (1775), clause ix.
30 25 Jan. 1775 (PB/Mins/1, p. 170).
31 26 June 1778 (PB/Mins/4, p. 230), 30 July 1779 (PB/Mins/6, p. 66).
32 29 Jan. 1774 (PB/Mins/1, p. 10).
33 6 June 1774 (PB/Mins/1, p. 3).
34 5 July 1780 (PB/Mins/7, p. 173).

The inspectors of nuisances often felt the direct wrath of unpopular decisions made by the Paving Board and the hazards and assaults they suffered plagued the Paving Board minute books from its earliest days. The work of physically mending and paving the streets of the city was performed by building contractors who were asked to supply samples of building materials and their proposals directly to the board.[35] They were overseen by supervisors of works and directly employed by the commissioners, and its repairs were planned and, once finished, measured by the Paving Board's surveyor.

Thomas Owen

Thomas Owen was elected as surveyor to the Dublin Paving Board on 29 June 1774 with an annual salary of £100.[36] His role, as mentioned in the introduction of this book, was to use measurement to quantify work completed on behalf of the Paving Board and to act as a technical advisor, ensuring that their duties were carried out to the highest possible standards.

Land surveying is the art of taking complex spatial measurements with highly accurate equipment and the conversion of such measurements into maps, plans, tables or charts. For Owen's role, the Paving Board required an individual who could determine the area of Dublin's streets, either singularly or over a neighbourhood, in square feet and inches. This figure would then be used to determine the amount and cost of paving and flagging required to improve the street, and thus the role of surveyor was central to both the body's long-term strategic plan to pave the city as well as determining the amount of revenue required to fulfil its goals. Maps were rarely, if ever, produced as part of this work as the Paving Board only required the area of the streets rather than knowing their layout. When mapping was required, it was usually adapted from commercially available, pre-existing maps of the city.

The surveying industry in 1770s Dublin consisted of roughly two dozen professionals, amateurs and part-time practitioners. It was an unregulated industry with no central authority or licensing system. There had been attempts by the surveyor general's office to rectify this during the 1750s by issuing certificates of proficiency to qualified practitioners but, with no supporting legislation to legally enforce these documents, they were simply viewed as professional references rather than official sanction to practice.[37] Land surveyors existed in a world that combined elements of engineering, architecture, construction and land valuation

---

35   18 June 1774 (PB/Mins/1, p. 7).

36   29 June 1774 (PB/Mins/1, p. 10).

37   The office of surveyor general was primarily concerned with civic engineering works around Ireland and not, despite its name, related to land surveying; Ó Cionnaith, *Mapping, measurement and metropolis*, p. 5.

in addition to core roles of geography, cartography and map production.[38] This dynamism also meant that practitioners of other fields, such as those with architectural and building backgrounds like Owen, could enter the industry with relative ease. Readily available survey treatises and manuals also assisted those with a background in measurement or mathematics to join the ranks of Dublin's surveyors.

There is no direct evidence of the instrumentation that Owen employed during this period to measure Dublin's streets, yet there are ways to speculate. Surveyors of the era were trained in the use of a wide array of instruments including the circumferentor[39] and the theodolite,[40] both used for angular measurement. However, both of these were of greater use on larger-scale surveys common on rural estates than the basic, short-distance linear measurements required by the Paving Board, indicating that the decimalised surveyor's chain and level would have been more apt for daily use.[41] The surveyor's chain (Fig. 1.2) was rather like a large steel measuring tape either 33ft or 66ft in length. Chains consisted of a series of links that were decimalised with markers every tenth link and required two people to hold either end, suggesting that Owen may have had an assistant for his paving work (although this is not mentioned in the historical record). By the late 1780s, he was known to have the help of his son in performing his daily survey duties;[42] however, his son appears to have only been a teenager during this time, so who provided Owen help during the 1770s remains unknown. The decimalisation of the chain via markers allowed measurements to be taken without the surveyor having to count every link in a chain close to thirty meters long, saving significant time. One Dublin practitioner praised this simple but useful adaptation, commenting that 'nothing could be more convenient' and the chain

---

38   Mary Colley, 'A list of architects, builders, surveyors, measurers and engineers extracted from Wilson's Dublin directories, 1760–1837', *IGSB*, 34 (1991), 7–68.

39   A surveyor's compass mounted on a tripod. Ó Cionnaith, *Mapping, measurement and metropolis*, p. 61; John Grey, *The art of land-measuring explained* (London, 1757); p. 273; Robert Gibson, *A treatise of practical surveying: which is demonstrated from its first principles* (Dublin, 1753), p. 148; Samuel Wyld, *The practical surveyor* (London, 1725), p. 55; Peter Callan, *A dissertation on the practice of land surveying in Ireland; and an essay towards a general regulation therein* (Drogheda, 1758), p. 32; J. Waddington, *A description of instruments used by surveyors: ... the practical method of finding the altitudes and distances of terrestrial objects. Land surveying, ... levelling, and the method of dividing land* (London 1773), p. 5.

40   John Hammond, *The practical surveyor: containing the most approved methods for the surveying of lands and waters ...* (London, 1765), p. 19; Gibson, *A treatise of practical surveying*, p. 160, Wyld, *The practical surveyor*, p. 66; Callan, *A dissertation*, p. 30.

41   Gibson, *A treatise of practical surveying*, p. 131; Wyld, *The practical surveyor*, p. 63; Benjamin Noble, *Geodesia Hibernica* (Dublin, 1768), p. 79; William Leybourn, *The works of Edmund Günter: containing the description and use of his sector, cross-staff, bow, quadrant, and other instruments ...* (London, 1662), p. 103; Adam Martindale, *The country survey book* (London, 1702), p. 26.

42   21 Feb. 1787 (PB/Mins/19, p. 272).

was highly popular among period Irish surveyors.[43] This decimalised method had been developed by Edmund Günter (1581–1626), professor of astronomy at Gresham College, England, and the term 'Günter's chain' was regularly used in period surveying manuals to describe the instrument.

As easy as they were to use, chains were not immune from fault. If the chain was stretched too tight between the surveyor and his assistant, the links in the chain were liable to stretch, thus causing a distortion in measurement. Conversely, if the tension in the chain was too lax it could also result in incorrect measurement due to sagging. Despite recommendations from period authors that the length of survey chains be regularly checked and adjusted,[44] such instrumentation problems were a regular source of conflict between rival surveyors not only in Dublin but across the island.[45] For smaller distances a solid ruler of several feet in length would have been sufficient.

1.2   Two men using a surveyor's chain (from Surveyors at work by an unknown artist (c.1800) (courtesy of the National Library of Ireland © NLI).

The eighteenth century was the golden era of the independent land surveyor in Ireland. Throughout the seventeenth century the role was often directly linked with English military campaigns around the country, as the forfeiture of estates and lands in the wake of revolts, rebellions and wars meant that there was a continual requirement for land measurement. From the 1820s onwards, the industry became dominated by the Ordnance Survey with levels of accuracy, technology and standardisation (not to mention financial backing) that individual

---

43   Noble, *Geodesia Hibernica*, p. 25.
44   Ibid., p. 79; Wyld, *The practical surveyor*, p. 79.
45   *Dublin Journal*, 16 Dec. 1749; ibid., 15 Aug. 1758; *Universal Advertiser*, 1 Dec. 1753; *Dublin Gazette*, 20 Sept. 1760.

Irish surveyors could not hope to match commercially. The eighteenth century therefore represents an era where a surveyor's success or failure was entirely dependent on his ability to obtain clients, produce high-quality results and stay ahead of competition in a cartographic free-for-all. Two of the city's primary pre-Ordnance Survey highpoints, namely Charles Brooking's *A map of the city and suburbs of Dublin* (Dublin, 1728) and John Rocque's masterpiece *An exact survey of the city and suburbs of Dublin* (Dublin, 1756), were produced during this period. Each represented the city at an important time of its development, with Rocque focusing on the minutia of the city's physical layout and Brooking providing insight into Dublin's civic and commercial administration. Rocque's map is reproduced in parts throughout this book.

In such a competitive market, and with many excellent surveyors practicing commercially, obtaining employment with an organisation such as the Paving Board was seen as a particularly lucrative position with secure and regular income. The Paving Board was not the only civic body concerned with improving Dublin during the latter eighteenth century to employ a full-time surveyor. The WSC, responsible for the construction of much of the modern layout of Dublin city centre, employed a number of surveyors from the 1750s onwards, including the highly successful and accomplished Thomas Sherrard, after whom Sherrard Street is named.[46] Other similar positions could be found in Dublin Corporation and the Ballast Board but they were relatively rare with most surveyors working in a private capacity.[47] These civic roles demonstrate that there was a distinct need from such bodies for precise geographic and technical information to achieve their goals. Though only an officer with the board, the surveyor's measurements played a core role in the administration, infrastructural development and financial efficiencies of the Paving Board. The duties of the surveyor were a key link joining the decisions made at the highest level of the paving commissioners directly to the board's employees and bank accounts and the citizens and streets of Dublin.

Frustratingly little is known about Owen outside of his professional life and there is no identified record of his image. He was an architect with experience in building[48] and was listed as a subscriber to the architectural works of both George Richardson's *Iconology; or, a collection of emblematical figures, moral and instructive* in 1779 and Pool and Cash's *Views of the most remarkable public buildings, monuments*

46   DCA WSC/Maps/41, 1789.
47   Ó Cionnaith, *Mapping, measurement and metropolis*, p. 31.
48   Brian Fitzgerald (ed.), *Correspondence of Emily, duchess of Leinster III* (Dublin, 1957).

and other edifices in the city of Dublin in 1780.[49] His marriage to Frances Darby in 1750 in St. Thomas parish, Dublin, allows his age when he commenced duties with the PB to be roughly estimated to around the mid-forties[50] and the couple had at least one son who was either very young or just born around 1774.[51] His name does not appear in street directories during his employment as surveyor to the Paving Board and his residence on North Cumberland Street is known only from a complaint made in 1783 by a contractor who was finding it difficult to track him down.[52]

Some background to his work outside of the PB is known, however these are only fleeting pieces of information. He was involved with a number of minor architectural alterations to Leinster House, Kildare Street, around 1780 producing designs for the kitchen wing, basement and second floors.[53] Owens work, though small, was quite prestigious considering the eminent architects who had also worked on the same building during this era, including Richard Castle (1690-1751), James Wyatt (1746-1813) and Isaac Ware (1704-66).[54] He also submitted designs for the Maynooth entrance and dog kennels at Carton House, Co. Kildare[55] however the greatest insight into both his work and personality are provided, thanks to the correspondence of Lady Emily Fitzgerald, duchess of Leinster (1731–1814; Fig. 1.3) and her sister Lady Louisa Conolly (1743–1821). This provides fascinating and highly luminous snippets of both his professional skill and his often trying personality. Between 1773 and 1776 Owen was employed by Emily at her residence in Frescati, Blackrock, Co. Dublin, for building, architecture and measurement work, and her impression of the man brings much of his subsequent work with the Paving Board into a far clearer light. Initially Lady Emily was keen to meet Owen, hoping he 'will turn out clever, for then he will be an amusement of the duke of Leinster';[56] however after several months she lamented on the slow rate of Owen's work.[57] Despite Owen's sluggishness he appears to have been quite skilled in his duties. Indeed two rare surviving architectural drawings he produced for the Maynooth gate at Carton House, Co. Kildare, and internal works

49   Robert Pool and John Cash, *Views of the most remarkable public buildings, monuments and other edifices in the city of Dublin* (Dublin, 1780), p. vi; George Richardson, *Iconology; or a collection of emblematical figures, moral and instructive* (London, 1779), p. viii.
50   Raymond Refausé (ed.), *Register of the parish of St. Thomas, Dublin 1750-1791* (RCB, 1994), p. 113.
51   21 Feb.1787 (PB/Mins/19, p. 269).
52   14 Feb. 1783 (PB/Mins/10, p. 184).
53   David Griffen and Caroline Pegum, *Leinster House 1744-2000, an architectural history* (IAA, 2000), p. ix, 4.
54   *Ibid*. p. 82.
55   *Ibid*.
56   Fitzgerald (ed.), *Correspondence of Emily*, p. 75.
57   Ibid., p. 88.

in Leinster House, Kildare Street, Dublin, were well executed and legible and give the impression of being created by a professional and highly capable hand (Figs 1.4 and 1.5). Accurate drawings, however, do not necessarily equate to a strong work ethic, financial sensibility or even a likable personality.

1.3   Emily Olivia Lennox, duchess of Leinster by Hugh Douglas Hamilton (c.1793). Pastel and graphite on paper (24.1 x 20cm). The duchess of Leinster was Thomas Owen's employer for a period during the 1770s (NGI 6088; photograph courtesy of the National Gallery of Ireland ©).

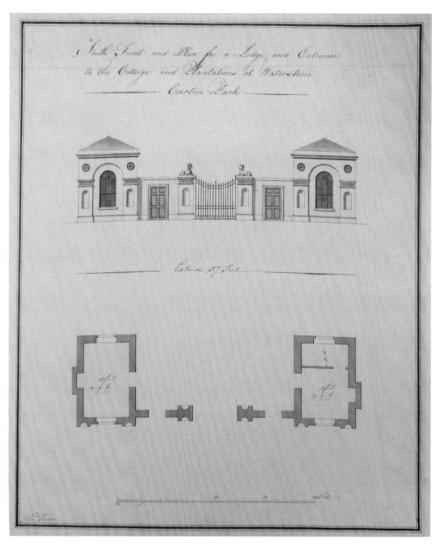

1.4   Thomas Owen's design for the Maynooth Gate of Carton House, Co. Kildare
       (c.1774) (courtesy of the Irish Architectural Archives ©).

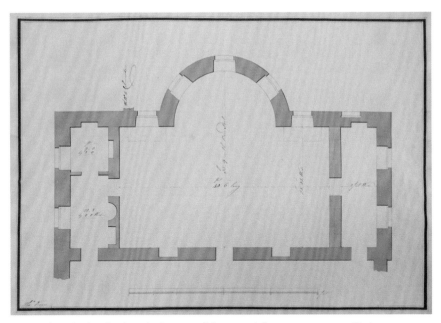

1.5   Owen's plan for the sub-division of the ground floor supper room of Leinster House, Dublin (c.1780). This design was never carried out and the room is now the Oireachtas Library (courtesy of the Irish Architectural Archives ©).

By the summer of 1775 a growing number of people were beginning to note that Owen's lack of speed may have less to do with perfectionism and more to do with laziness, as mentioned by Lady Louisa:

> Mr Owens [sic] assured me that all the doors and architraves were ready. He was to proceed on repairing the old part of the house this week ... I find that people seem to think that Owens has been idle about your house, and I am sure I am no judge whether that is true or not; but I hope it is not, for I have actually seen a vast deal of work ready, and hope that the chief necessary expense is over.[58]

Adding a number of weeks later: 'Owens is very tiresome, for we cannot get a plan of the cellar floor which Sarah wrote to him for a month ago'.[59] Around this time a worrying number of comments were made between the two sisters about Owen and his financial demands. He was already employed by the Paving Board and receiving his £100 salary from them, yet there appeared to be a growing distrust by the sisters about his honestly on monetary matters:

---

58   Lady Louisa Conolly to Duchess of Leinster; ibid., p. 138.
59   Ibid., p. 145.

I have heard nothing of Owens since the £200 he got.[60]

Mr Owens has now had, since you left Ireland, £1,385–2–0; and I imagine must have about £500 more before it's done. He does go on, but not so fast as I could wish. The only comfort is that Mr Ward says it's well done.[61]

I do long very much to have that *leech* Mr Owens turned off, who really sucks your *vitals*, and the drains from your poor pocket are a great trouble to me.[62]

I have quite a dread of giving him an order for money when I am in England, after what Mr Ogilvie says of him.[63]

Owens is tiresome to the last degree, but he has really executed the work well.[64]

Whether being referred to as a 'leech' is justifiable, it must be noted that his delay in supplying work and financial peculiarities were not restricted to his employment at Frescati as similar problems reappeared a number of times in the pages of the Paving Board minute books.[65] From the above quotes it is possible to assume that perhaps Owen's simultaneous work with the Paving Board and for the duchess of Leinster may have overextended his capabilities and he was having problems allocating appropriate time to achieve a balance between his duties. Similar issues were not uncommon for other surveyors of the same era. Fellow practitioner Jacob Neville encountered such large financial issues while trying to complete a survey of County Wicklow in 1761 that he lost his home,[66] and the first holder of the title Dublin City Surveyor, John Greene Jr, was 'often out of town when he is wanted'[67] while trying to balance his official civic responsibilities and maintain a private business at the same time. There is evidence, however, that Owen's personality, rather than poor time management, may have played a role in souring the opinions

60   29 Aug. 1775; Ibid., p. 147.
61   13 Sept. 1775; Ibid., p. 150.
62   23 Nov. 1775; Ibid., p. 159.
63   William Ogilvie was tutor to the duke of Leinster's younger children and was resident in Blackrock. 7 Dec. 1775 and 10 Mar. 1776; ibid., pp 54, 160.
64   Ibid., p. 206.
65   26 Sept. 1776 (PB/Mins/2, p. 208); 8 Apr. 1780 (PB/Mins/7, p. 50); 14 Feb. 1783 (PB/Mins/10, p. 184); 19 Apr. 1783 (PB/Mins/10, p. 256).
66   *Dublin Journal*, 12 Mar. 1761.
67   24 Apr. 1698; J.T. Gilbert (ed.), *Calendar of ancient records of Dublin in the possession of the municipal corporation*, vi, p. 196.

of those around him. By the autumn of 1775 the two sisters were beginning to suspect that Owen had been openly lying to them regarding letters that he claimed were lost and that he may in fact have been trying to deceive them:

> But you frighten me and surprise me about Owens [*sic*], and cannot think why he tells me so many lies, or is so unfortunate as to have all his letters lost; for he assured me that he had lately sent you all his accounts up to Michaelmas, and the drawings for your chimney-pieces ages ago, as likewise that for your kitchen and scullery ... William [Ogilvie] never let me into the secret that he had a bad opinion of him, as often as we have talked over your expenses at the Black Rock. And whether he had cheated you or not, God knows, and is quite out of my power to know. Mr Ward's approving of the work is my only comfort and he did seem to think you had the worth of your money. However, at Xmas I hope (as I told you in my last) that Owens will have finish'd so as to be dismissed.[68]

Again we return to the contrasting world of Thomas Owen – well executed and professional work but with disturbing questions over his honesty and inability to get on with those around him. His role with the Paving Board also supports this hypothesis, with evidence of a significant personal dispute with a commissioner where Owen appeared to be the transgressor occurring in June 1777, only three years after joining the Paving Board as surveyor.

All human beings have innate flaws and Thomas Owen was no exception. Whether he was lazy, had a short temper, difficult personality or social eccentricities can only be speculated on, but what can be concluded is that the letters between Lady Louisa Conolly and Lady Emily Fitzgerald give rare and valuable insight into the life of Owen not recorded in the detailed but sterile minute books of the Paving Board.

The surveyor of the Paving Board (1774)

Elections for the position of surveyor to the Dublin Paving Board were held in late June 1774.[69] In the paving act passed by parliament, the duties of the surveyor were listed quite generally, lacking much of the detail that the role would eventually require:

---

68   22 Oct. 1775; Fitzgerald (ed.), *Correspondence of Emily*, p. 157.
69   29 June 1774 (PB/Mins/1, p. 10).

[The surveyor will] view the condition of the several streets, quays, bridges, squares, courts, alleys, places and lanes of the said city of Dublin ... and to see that the same are properly pitched, paved and kept in repair.[70]

Three names were initially submitted for the role: Thomas Owen, Thomas Mathews (active 1754–82) and William Cox (active 1767–80). Both Mathews and Cox were land surveyors, which differed from Owen's mixed background of building and architecture.

Mathews had been operating in Dublin since the 1750s[71] as an assistant to the then-official city surveyor and dean of St Patrick's Cathedral, Roger Kendrick (active 1735; d. 1779), who he replaced in 1764.[72] The office of City Surveyor was a position held within Dublin Corporation that was responsible for providing the corporation with all its mapping and measurement requirements, primarily relating to land and leases held by the city. It was the highest civic office that existed for surveyors in Dublin and was held by at least eleven individuals from its origin in the 1670s until it was dissolved in 1857.[73] Mathews could thus be held as the senior surveyor for all of Dublin and this role would have led him to have direct contact with the government of the city on a regular basis. One important aspect of his tenure in this role was the compilation of a single collection of all surviving maps and records of the office of city surveyor since its foundation, thus marking a major milestone in cartographic conservation for the city of Dublin.[74]

Less is known about the other contender William Cox. Cox was an estate surveyor with his maps often being distinguishable by the use of a decorative human hand pointing north instead of a more traditional north arrow or compass rose.[75] Estate surveyors specialised in producing maps of large areas using instruments such as a circumferentor or theodolite[76] and their maps were often accompanied by detailed portfolios of field areas used to determine the agricultural output of land (and thus the potential rental value a landlord could charge his tenants). Cox, like other land surveyors, was therefore used to dealing with complex projects with tight timelines to supply correct information to wealthy and powerful individuals.

---

70   15 & 16 Geo. III, c. 20 [Ire.] (1775), clause xii.
71   Dublin city surveyors' book of maps (DCA C1.S1.69).
72   4 May 1764; Gilbert (ed.), *Calendar of ancient records*, xi, p. 208.
73   Ó Cionnaith, *Mapping, measurement and metropolis*, p. 175.
74   11 Apr. 1766; Gilbert (ed.), *Calendar of ancient records*, xi, pp 326–7.
75   Ó Cionnaith, *Mapping, measurement and metropolis*, p. 175.
76   Ibid., p. 148 [circumferentor]; ibid., p. 160 [theodolite].

Owen won the election to the office of Paving Board surveyor.[77] But why did Owen, with no known recorded history of surveying, win the election against two professional, experienced and well-regarded competitors? The role of surveyor to the Paving Board required a mixture of construction and building skill on top of what would now be considered engineering surveying. The surveyor was primarily responsible for identifying methods that the Paving Board could use to achieve its goals,[78] taking height levels of paving work conducted,[79] supervising construction sites,[80] evaluating the quality of material used by the Paving Board[81] and, perhaps most importantly, calculating the area of paving laid, thus determining the cost of such work.[82] This role could therefore be more accurately defined as falling somewhere between that of a conventional land surveyor and that of a 'measurer', an eighteenth-century title for one skilled in the art of determining areas and volumes (and thus cost) of construction projects, and an engineer.[83] Perhaps it was Owen's background in building and architecture, coupled with his association with the duchess of Leinster, that gave him a competitive edge over Mathews and Cox. Owen is recorded as having given testimony many years later to some of his more technical duties as surveyor, far detached from traditional land surveying, through the assignment of labour to the board's supervisors of work (in essence district foremen), regarding building and construction responsibilities:

> That as surveyor of the corporation, the duty of the supervisors does in some respect come under his inspection ... that he gives the supervisors directions for laying out the footpaths; & that the supervisors attend him to receive those instructions: that the supervisors see orders executed, & that long lines or sections are also executed.[84]

This technical supervision may have perhaps been beyond Mathews and Cox, but the key duty undertaken by the board's surveyor was not – the measurement of paving work done by contractors either with measure rule or surveyor's chain. Contractors were employed to do much of the construction work for the Paving Board. Once their work had been completed, the surveyor would inspect its quality

---

77   29 June 1774 (PB/Mins/1, p. 10).
78   Ibid.
79   19 May 1775 (PB/Mins/1, p. 255).
80   28 Sept. 1776 (PB/Mins/2, p. 227).
81   13 Dec. 1782 (PB/Mins/10, p. 156).
82   12 May 1780 (PB/Mins/6, p. 94).
83   P. Levi Hodgson, *The modern measurer, particularly adapted to timber and building, according to the present standard of the kingdom of Ireland* (Dublin, 1793); William Hawney, *The complete measurer; or the whole art of measuring* (London, 1730).
84   8 Aug. 1777 (PB/Mins/3, p. 212).

and calculate the area in square yards and feet, which was used to then determine the value of their work done.[85] Unfortunately for Owen, some of his more unpleasant work habits first encountered at Frescati would re-emerge directly relating to such measurement work and his financial dealings with the paving contractors. This would see him brought up on serious charges before his employers several years later and sheds light on some questionable attributes he brought to the role.[86]

While Thomas Mathews would continue his work as Dublin City surveyor until his death in 1782,[87] the 1774 election would not be the last time that Owen would have to compete for his job and it would not be the last dealing he would have with William Cox.

---

85   Hawney, *The complete measurer*, p. 253.
86   19 Aug. 1783 (PB/Mins/10, p. 256).
87   17 Oct. 1782; Gilbert (ed.), *Calendar of ancient records*, xii, p. 261.

2 Paving Dublin's streets (1774–82)

With its basic administrative structure established and its officer positions filled by individuals the board saw as fit, the Paving Board, with Sydenham Singleton (d. 1800) as chairman, could now begin work in amending some of Dublin's more pressing street issues. This was a major city-wide undertaking to commence at once, so in order to best deploy its resources the Paving Board first needed to identify and prioritise problems across the city – in essence a stocktaking exercise in urban infrastructure.

Mapping played a central role in these early days of the board by acting as a platform through which a coherent strategy could be formed. Major Charles Vallancey, commissioner for the third division and a military engineer/surveyor of some note, supplied the board with a divisional map of the city mounted on canvas from which it could plan its business and identify the often complex divisional borders snaking through the heart of Dublin.[88] On a more local level, Owen was requested on the day of his election to supply the Paving Board with 'such [a] plan, as he thinks will most facilitate the proceedings of the corporation, and which shall appear to him to be the most economical to be adopted'.[89] In addition to each division being asked to locate problems, poorly maintained streets and places lacking footpaths within their respective areas. Of paramount importance was the identification and removal of street nuisances including

> all signs, sign irons, posts whether of wood or stone, spur stones, landing stones, boards, bulks, show glasses, show boards, set out windows & penthouses in the city ... [being] nuisances at present subsisting in the several streets, lanes and alleys of this city.[90]

The members of the Paving Board were all residents of Dublin so they would have had a basic knowledge of the state of the city from their interactions therein. However, they were not in an informed position to comment on what streets were in need of attention in every part of the city and depended instead on the reports from the city's parishes. Over the course of several weeks, a more accurate picture of Dublin's streets began to be revealed in the Paving Board meetings. Several major streets in the first and second divisions were initially identified as having significant problems, particularly along the Dorset Street–Capel Street axis. A sewer on North Great Georges Street was causing so great a nuisance that 'the ground in said street being raised in such a manner as to greatly annoy

---

88   5 July 1774 (PB/Mins/1, p. 20).
89   29 June 1774 (PB/Mins/1, p. 12).
90   14 June 1774 (PB/Mins/1, p. 5).

the inhabitants of Great Britain Street [modern Parnell Street] by overflowing the same', there were breaches in the quay wall on Liffey Street[91] and flooding on Great Ship Street.[92] The city's ability to operate in an effective commercial manner was also being impeded by 'block stones, mills stones, boards, balks & other heavy lumber' acting as obstructions for ships docking along some of the most important areas of the south quays,[93] while that eternal traffic black spot, College Green, was noted as having considerable issues.[94]

Paving was central to the board's work. Its primary goal was to achieve a level of quality paving throughout the city so as to improve transportation and the living conditions of its residents. As vital as this task was, the commissioners were also aware that the product of their labours would be highly visible to the general public, thus placing their work under constant city-wide scrutiny.

The process of laying pavement was relatively straight forward. With few underground utilities present during the period, apart from sewers, water pipes and drains, little preparatory work was required for the contracted builders. First the existing surface was removed, a level bed of compacted coarse gravel was set (to allow for water drainage) and covered with a layer of sand that helped hold the paving stones in place. Ideally the paving stones, often sourced from quarries in Wicklow, would have straight edges so as to form a tight seal with their neighbour; the Paving Board came in for criticism, however, for reusing rough and unsuitable old paving slabs on occasion.[95] Harder flagging material was utilised for the road kerb and the board went to great length to try and ensure that its contractors' work was well executed before they were paid. One issue of concern came from the possibility of a poorly laid gravel foundation, often directly onto unprotected subsoil or made vulnerable to water due to a lack of suitable surface protection (see p. 127). This could cause substantial problems as the weight of carts and carriages using the road could cause movement in the gravel and distort the joins between paving slabs, warping the road or street. One period commentator thought that this problem was a frequent issue with the Paving Board's work, 'hence the holes we see in every street'.[96]

---

91   5 July 1774 (PB/Mins/1, p. 17).
92   15 July 1774 (PB/Mins/1, p. 27).
93   26 July 1774 (PB/Mins/1, p. 37).
94   9 Sept. 1774 (PB/Mins/1, p. 78).
95   *Dublin Evening Post*, 8 Apr. 1784.
96   Anon., *Observations on the paving acts: reports, execution of works, &c., addressed to those whom it may concern* (Dublin, 1782), p. 49.

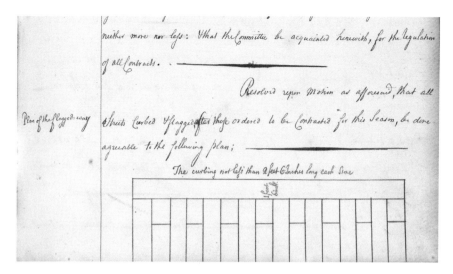

2.1   A sketch of a section of pavement found in the Paving Board minute book for 1778 (DCA/PB/Mins/4, p. 134) (courtesy of Dublin City Library and Archives).

With the eyes of the Dublin on them, public relations was a key focus for the Paving Board to achieve its goals. In 1774 alone, ten thousand handbills were printed and distributed door-to-door across the city asking residents to comply with the body. Each household was asked that

> no window shall project over the flagged path more than 3 inches
> at the cill ... [and] no ornament, cornice, entablature, architrave,
> or mouldings of any kind over the said windows or doors, shall
> project more than 6 inches.[97]

The specificity contained in these handbills, while seeming somewhat extreme, is testament to the length of control that the Paving Board sought over the city's buildings, all of which was legally enforceable with fines and prison sentences. It was becoming clear to Dublin's residents that this new regime was going to have a significant impact on their daily lives.

Understandably, there were those who objected to such requests and the subsequent trouble it would cause them to alter their homes and businesses to see that the Paving Board's somewhat overzealous rules were followed. In a newspaper article from July 1774, addressed directly to Paving Board chairman Sydenham Singleton, a resident of the city expressed his disbelief that the initial requests from the Paving Board seemed so far removed from what the public's perception of the organisation had been:

---

97   *Freeman's Journal*, 9 July 1774.

The act of parliament, by which the commissioners have their power, was originally intended to remove nuisances. Give me leave to define a nuisance; in my humble opinion, it is whatever *incommodes, obstructs or injures the publick* ... That jet out windows are a nuisance in many places is universally granted; but then it is only in narrow streets and passages that even *they* are nuisances. But I will give it up, for argument sake, that jet-out's are nuisances everywhere: take the ornaments over the windows, that are situated from 10 to 14 feet above the foot way a nuisance? How do they either *incommodes, obstructs or injures the publick?*[98]

By having to remove decorative features from the front of buildings far above street level, the author accused the Paving Board of not being the solvers of nuisances but in fact the creators of them:

Should you oblige [citizens] to take down their ornaments, which have cost from 30 to 100 guineas each, what recompense will you make them? If none, what are they worth when taken down? ... But are not decorations of this kind an ornament to the streets of business and a beauty to the city? Did ever any number of sensible men before determine, that what was an ornament to the city, and no way *even* inconvenience to the publick should be removed merely because it was a project of 12 instead of 6 inches?[99]

The unknown author, in a somewhat malicious note against his fellow citizens, concluded his request for leniency by stating that if there was no means to alter Singleton's opinion or the rules or the Paving Board, that they should first direct their attention to the bow windows of Mr Dennis Serjeant on St Stephens Green, who appears to have been an adversary.

The points raised in this article did indeed make sense. A universal ban on façade ornamentation would only result in less public support for the Paving Board's requests and the response to the requested statement was accommodating. The commissioners fully agreed that projections or ornaments well above the public thoroughfare, or at a lower level where the street was very wide, and causing no

---

98   Ibid.
99   Ibid.

obstruction, should be exempt, giving parts of Parliament Street and Capel Street as examples. In allowing such accommodation the Paving Board were following the guidance set down by their London equivalent where

> on the Strand (the broad part) Fleet Street; Cheapside; Charring Cross, &c. &c. &c. where even jet out windows, show-glasses, &c. area admitted, the streets being sufficiently broad to answer the several purposes of the public, independent of those *private* accommodations.[100]

2.2   The Tholsel, Skinners Row, Dublin by James Malton (1792). Ink and watercolour (42.4 x 58.8cm). The Tholsel served as a meeting point for the Dublin Paving Board during the 1770s (NGI 2185; photograph courtesy of the National Gallery of Ireland ©).

An ironic consequence of the Paving Board's enthusiasm in enforcing its nuisance policy was that they fell victim to their own rules. From July 1774, the commissioners met regularly at the city Tholsel on Christchurch Place (Fig. 2.2)[101] where, a few weeks after moving to the premises, they were forced to complain to the lord mayor that the building where they fined people for not removing nuisances was in fact a nuisance in its own right as '[the steps and pillars] will prove an obstruction to the intended footpaths & ought to be removed'.[102] Despite their

---

100   Ibid.
101   1 July 1774 (PB/Mins/1, p. 10).
102   19 Aug. 1774 (PB/Mins/1, p. 52).

willingness to bend some rules in the name of common sense and the appeasement of the public, the commissioners were not above making examples of some of the city's residents who refused to cooperate with them as a lesson to others. The first fine ever issued by the Paving Board was to a Mr Waller of Capel Street, whose projecting windows at his linen drapery business were noted as being in violation of the commissioners' orders, and he was found to have treated the board 'with great insolence'.[103] Matters only grew worst once the local division supervisor and two carpenters were sent to take the windows down, with Waller physically resisting them and threatening to pull the men off their ladders if they continued. He was fined twice – once for refusing to cooperate and once for assaulting the commissioners' employees.[104] Indeed records about physical violence, threats and aggressive mobs litter the commissioners' minutes from the date of the Paving Board's foundation (see p. 60). The daily aggression from Dubliners towards this body paints a vivid picture of the world that the Paving Board operated in at street level and is examined in more detail later in this chapter.

College Green (Fig. 2.3), at the busy junction of Grafton Street, Dame Street and, prior to the construction of Westmoreland Street, College Street, was one of the earliest priorities of the Paving Board. The junction was a traffic nightmare, with two large and busy institutions (Trinity College and the Irish Parliament House) facing onto it. It was also the beginning of the main east–west thoroughfare on the south side of the city. These issues were greatly added to by the narrowness of the surrounding streets, resulting in traffic bottlenecks, particularly when parliament was sitting. In September 1774, the commissioners had the following notice published in order to reduce traffic congestion and to help keep the city flowing:

> As Dame Street is now open'd for carriages, the corporation request that the following rule be observed here as in London to avoid confusion & obstruction. That all carriages going towards College Green shall pass right [left crossed out] hand side of the street, & all carriages going from College Green towards Cork Hill do also pass on the right [left crossed out again] hand side of the street.[105]

103   *Leinster Journal*, 12 Sept. 1774.
104   Ibid.
105   9 Sept. 1774 (PB/Mins/1, p. 78).

2.3   View of the Parliament House, College Green, Dublin by James Malton (1793).
       College Green was one of the first areas of the city to which the Paving Board
       turned its attention (courtesy of the National Library of Ireland © NLI).

The notice continued with a polite appeal to the city's upper classes who wished to socialise on the green:

> The corporation also request that no gentleman or lady will stop at the door of any house in the said street in their carriages; but that they will please to alight, & order their carriages to stand in any one of the collateral streets, or more on the length of the street in the suit of the other carriages, until they shall be ready to be taken up.[106]

This notice may perhaps be one of the earliest traffic management plans for Dublin city centre. Yet despite their best intentions, the area remained a significant nuisance and, by the early 1780s, the lord mayor issued an order that no traffic would be allowed on College Green during the sitting of parliament and with those who violated the order facing significant consequences (much like the modern College Green Bus Corridor plan):[107]

---

106   Ibid.
107   A traffic management plan initiated in 2009 and enforced by members of the Gardaí that
      restricts traffic to public transport vehicles and taxis through College Green during morning
      and evening rush hour.

And I do hereby require all persons whatsoever to take notice thereof at their peril; and the High Constable and the several Constables of this city are desired to attend from time to time, and enforce this proclamation.[108]

Possibly one of the most lasting legacies of the initial work of the Paving Board still felt in Dublin today was its work on street signs and house numbers. Dublin had far surpassed a point where local knowledge would be sufficient to navigate the entire the city, thus necessitating signposts. The spread of postage and the increase in new neighbourhoods throughout the city also meant that house numbering was becoming increasingly important. The commissioners informed the inhabitants of Dublin that all houses were to be numbered and

> may also order and direct to be engraved, painted, or otherwise described on stone or wood, to be fixed on a conspicuous part of some house or other building at each end or corner of each square, street, or lane, the name by which said square, street or lane is usually or properly called or known.[109]

2.4   The Tholsel, Skinners Row, Dublin by James Malton (1792) (detail). Ink and watercolour (42.4 x 58.8cm). Street signs and house numbers became mandatory for Dublin under the Paving Board's rulings. Sedan chairs, such as the one pictured on the pavement, also felt the impact of the board. (NGI 2185; photograph courtesy of the National Gallery of Ireland ©).

---

108   *Freeman's Journal*, 9 Mar. 1782.
109   15 & 16 Geo. III, c. 20 [Ire.] (1775), clause xxvi.

Failure to comply with house numbering or vandalism of street signs was a finable offence, with offenders being charged up to five shillings.[110] This desire to name Dublin's streets brings up a question about urban environments: is it necessary to be literate in order to navigate a city? The medieval origins of many of the street names in Dublin such as Winetavern Street, Fishable Street and Castle Street reflect the original business practiced therein. However, over many centuries, these businesses can relocate or disappear, thus removing the obvious visual hints as to the street's name. Through street signage and house numbering, the desire from the Paving Board for urban conformity and modernisation can be seen as a consequence of increasing levels of literacy among Dublin's population and the requirement that a stranger to the city (of which in a bustling port there would be many) could correctly navigate their way simply by being able to read.

Financing Dublin's streets

As progressive as these early initiatives were, the Paving Board required significant income and financial management during its formative years. Indeed its finances, rather than its service provision, would often be the most contentious issue regarding this body and one that would come back to haunt it again and again.

The first treasurer to the Paving Board, John Finlay (d. 1823), was elected at the same meeting that saw Owen appointed as surveyor.[111] All money received by the commissioners through taxation and grants would be held at the bank of Thomas Finlay & Co. and a funds committee consisting of fifteen members was established to see how best to finance their work.[112] David LaTouche Jr (1726–1816), an influential member of the Irish parliament with strong connections to the banking industry and described by Paving Board secretary Gladwell as 'one who is ever attentive to promote the public good',[113] offered the commissioners an advance of £1,000 per division. An initial £100 was given to each parochial committee for repairs, while the remaining £900 was kept for the paving and flagging of main streets in each division. This initial funding allowed the divisions to take on their own paid staff including clerks (£10 per annum), supervisors of works (£22 5s. per annum)[114] and even a caretaker for the board's main office who was paid £2 a quarter 'for keeping the room of meeting clean, attending & providing fire'.[115]

---

110   1 July 1774 (PB/Mins/1 p. 14); 19 Aug. (PB/Mins/1, p. 53).
111   29 June 1774 (PB/Mins/1, p. 10).
112   5 July 1774 (PB/Mins/1, p. 18).
113   Evidence of Robert Thorp; report by the Rt Hon. Sir John Blaquiere (1784), quoted in LaTouche, et al., *Report of the commissioners*, p. 234.
114   26 July 1774 (PB/Mins/1, p. 35).
115   22 Dec. 1780 (PB/Mins/8, p. 51).

Paving taxes levied against each building in the Paving Board's jurisdiction were charged at 12 pence in a pound of annual rent for houses, shops, warehouses and vaults, while churches, churchyards, chapels, meeting houses and public buildings were taxed 4 pence per square yard. Tenants were liable to pay the paving tax, not the property owner, and unoccupied buildings were charged at a half rate.[116] If a resident did not pay their tax within ten days of being informed that it was due by a note 'or demand in writing left at the place of abode', Paving Board collectors were empowered to enter residences with parish constables and remove belongings of the same value as the money owed.[117] If such belongings could not be produced or if the resident refused to allow access to the collectors, they could be imprisoned for between ten days and two months.[118]

Divisional incomes from taxation varied across the city, largely depending on the value of the property and the number of buildings present in each. An audit conducted by the Paving Board in 1780 provides an overview of the total paving tax collected against that which was due for each division:

Table 1.1 Taxes owed and collected by the Paving Board from 1774 to 1780. Note: the sixth and seventh divisions were incorporated in 1776.

Division	Building (tax income)	Dead wall/void spaces (tax income)	Total due to receive per year	Collected since 1774	Average per year
1	£845 10s. 7d.	£361 7s. 3d.	£1215 17s. 10d.	£4942 19s. 10d.	£908 11s. 11d.
2	£1206 2s. 4d.	£235 12s. 8d.	£1441 15s. 1/2d.	£6318 3s. 7d.	£1263 12s. 8d.
3	£1950 11s. 0d.	£449 12s. 2d.	£2399 11s. 2d.	£8779 13s.	£1755 18s. 7d.
4	£1139 11s. 6d.	£86 15s. 4d.	£1225 15s. 10d.	£4849 8s. 1d.	£969 17s. 1d.
5	£1043 3s. 4d.	£129 17s. 3d.	£1173 15s. 7 1/2d.	£4804 18s. 5d.	£960 19s. 8d.
6	£194 4s. 3d.	£50 17s. 10d.	£248 2s. 1d.	£361 14s. 8d.	£144 13s. 10d.
7	£308 13s. 0d.	£78 9s. 1d.	£287 2s. 1d.	£206 7s. 3d.	£82 10s. 11d.
Total	£6599 5s. 0d.	£1391 19s. 8d.	£7991 4s. 8d.	£30263 4s. 11d.	£6166 5s. 3d.

According to this data, no division was receiving the amount of tax income it was due year-to-year and the entire organisation was losing roughly the modern equivalent of several hundred thousands of euro per annum in uncollected taxes. This represented a significant financial deficit in a body that was, in theory, supposed to be entirely self funded and was an issue that would come back to haunt the Paving Board.

---

116   15 & 16 Geo. III, c. 20 [Ire.] (1775), clauses xxxix and xl.
117   Ibid., clause xlii.
118   Ibid., clause xx.

One cause of this deficit was the problems regularly encountered when the Paving Board went to collect its tax. The commissioners' tax collectors (on commission at 6*d*. per pound collected) were responsible for visiting each premises in their respective divisions and ensuring that all money owed to the Paving Board was paid. This proved to be a difficult and often dangerous role that frequently put them in the direct line of fire from citizens who aggressively resented paying the tax. To counteract their substantial losses, the Paving Board started borrowing extensively. It was this decision, coupled with extensive financial mismanagement, that ultimately led to the board's disgrace in the early 1780s (see p. 64). In London, the local Paving Board would undertake a cost estimate for paving based on their surveyors' measurements and would wait until they had sufficient funds before commencing work. Unfortunately for Dublin 'this prudent example our commissioners despised and rejected'.[119] Under statute, the Paving Board was only allowed to borrow one third of its income annually. Secretary Richard Gladwell estimated that this should have limited loans to around £2,000 a year; however the commissioners felt that this was not acceptable as their own estimates suggested that up to £6,200 a year would need to be spent on their work.[120] Two years after LaTouche's initial £5,000 loan, the Paving Board borrowed a staggering £15,000, followed by an additional £4,000 the following year.[121] Given its inability to recover their losses from taxation, it had managed to dig itself into a fiscal hole from which it would ultimately not be able to escape.

Borrowed or not, how the Paving Board's income was spent depended substantially on the role of Thomas Owen and his measurements. His impact on the budget of the funds committee can be seen in one of his very first major paving projects. In July 1774 he was asked to 'lay before this committee the level of Dame Street from end to end together with his opinion on how the same shall be regulated',[122] in addition to calculating the necessary number of square yards for pavement and square feet for flagging. Owen's measurements determined that 1,575 square yards for paving and 7,954 square feet of flagging were required for Dame Street (Fig. 2.5), estimated at a cost of £350.[123] Contractors were then hired; in this case paver John Kelner supplied paving at 2 1/2 pence per yard, while the flagging was done by stonecutter Arthur Backton at 9 pence per yard.[124]

119 Evidence of Robert Thorp; quoted in LaTouche, et al., *Report of the commissioners*, p. 235.
120 Evidence of Richard Gladwell; ibid., p. 231.
121 Ibid.
122 26 July 1774 (PB/Mins/1, p. 38).
123 26 July 1774 (PB/Mins/1, p. 39).
124 5 Aug 1774 (PB/Mins/1, p. 43).

2.5   Dame Street (from John Rocque, An exact survey of the city of Dublin (1756), courtesy of the Board of Trinity College Dublin).

While the 1774 work on Dame Street provides a good example of a single street project that linked the Paving Board's finances to Owen's work, he could also assist the funds committee with trying to calculate future cost estimates over a much wider region. He was called upon several times a year to supply area measurements of each street that had been identified by a divisional committee as requiring repair in the upcoming season.[125] His opinion on material quality was also sought as this again had to come from the commissioners' coffers.[126] These predetermined estimates allowed the funds committee to adjust its budget in advance of work taking place and highlights the overall strategic plan the Paving Board attempted to implement to maintain Dublin's streets.

Fines issued by the Paving Board not only provided the commissioners with additional income but played the simultaneous role of asserting the Paving Board's civic authority while ensuring that its decrees were complied with. Early in the Paving Board's work the parochial committee of St Werburgh's sought clarification on how they should act as

> This committee almost every morning observes in different parts of this division quantities of rubbish & filth of different sorts are laid in the streets: Therefore ordered that the clerk do lay before the commissioners the above complaint, & request their directions how the offenders may be punished for the same.[127]

The commissioners decided that a fine of 5 shillings should be applied to every offence and it should be issued every day until each nuisance was removed. Other fines, from 20 shillings up to £5, could also be levied against citizens for opening

---

125   14 May 1779 (PB/Mins/6, p. 18); 12 May 1780 (PB/Mins/7, p. 90).
126   12 May 1780 (PB/Mins/6, p. 90).
127   7 Oct. 1774 (PB/Mins/1, p. 106).

pavement to lay water pipes without permission,[128] leaving nuisances on the street[129] or non-payment of taxes.[130] Retrieving these fines could prove difficult, however, as one collector lamented that 'it is hard to bear being called [a] robber, rascal and insolent scoundrel, for merely calling at a man's door, & telling him he is fined for not having the footway cleansed'.[131] Aside from the paving tax and fines, revenue could be generated by the Paving Board in a number of ways. Residents along the Liffey were required to pay for the raising and maintenance of quay walls in front of their property,[132] while additional loans could be borrowed from other government organisations that might have overlapping areas of interest, as when the Barrack Board lent £2,000 for new pavement from Church Street to what is now Collins Barracks.[133]

Despite the frequent financial difficulties that the commissioners encountered, their duties still had to be carried out. By the autumn of 1774, the Paving Board had commenced in earnest their detailed work in applying order to Dublin's street life. Yet their financial problems would hound them throughout their existence and ultimately lead to collapse, scandal and failure.

Dublin's street life

The Dublin Paving Commissioners' work was in essence both macro- and micro-management of the city's streets. Large engineering and administration works, such as the substantial repaving of Dame Street or the enforcement of house numbering were offset with what sometimes appear to be trivial, almost petty, complaints about items as small as a sack of potatoes or cushions causing a street nuisance.[134] This body dealt with all levels of Dublin's society in an often turbulent world, trying to establish a long-term strategic plan while dealing with daily annoyances and complaints from Dublin's diverse citizenry in an era of rapid growth and urban change.

As the board's work was conducted outdoors, seasonal variations in weather conditions could have a major impact. Major paving repair work could only be undertaken during the drier months of the year and the period from November to February was designated for temporary or emergency work only.[135] Apart from

---

128   31 May 1776 (PB/Mins/2, p. 222); 13 May 1778 (PB/Mins/4, p. 69).
129   14 Oct. 1784 (PB/Mins/16, p. 161).
130   6 June 1783 (PB/Mins/10, p. 310).
131   15 Dec. 1784 (PB/Mins/13, p. 210).
132   4 Aug. 1775 (PB/Mins/1, p. 314); 15 & 16 Geo. III, c. 20 [Ire.] (1775), clauses lxii.
133   17 Nov. 1775 (PB/Mins/1, p. 370).
134   21 Sept. 1785 (PB/Mins/16, p. 91) ; 11 Apr. 1785 (PB/Mins/14, p. 245).
135   28 Feb. 1777 (PB/Mins/3, p. 37).

paving, the Paving Board was also tasked with trying to apply a form of order to the often chaotic life on Dublin streets. One of the primary issues that the commissioners noted as public nuisances were the city's many congested and dirty market areas, found primarily in the medieval core of the city and in western and southern neighbourhoods. Attempts had been made by the corporation in the 1680s to improve the condition of many of Dublin's markets. Under a series of edicts, streets in market areas were to be kept free of blockages, street butchers and bakers were to be removed from Fishable Street and High Street respectively and shops were to be kept clean with limited signage. Permanent shops were preferable to stalls as they did not hinder traffic as much and reduced waste build-up in the middle of streets.[136] These measures, despite being logical and to the benefit of the greater city, were ultimately unsuccessful and by the late eighteenth century Dublin's markets were again causing significant traffic problems (Fig. 2.6). For the Paving Board, the meat and root markets on Thomas Street and Patrick Street were found to be problematic by their local divisional committee, primarily due to poorly placed stalls that caused significant street blockages and limiting movement. The market community, sensing their territory was about to be infringed, were quick to offer resistance to the board. Stall owners, particularly from the butchers' market on Patrick Street, argued that their existing set-up was nothing new to the city and that the area 'hath been time immoral a butchers' market',[137] while the earl of Meath stated vehemently that he had a patent from the reign of Charles II allowing his family to run a meat market on Meath Street.[138] Despite such protests, the commissioners were determined to exert their control over these areas. Their war on Dublin's main markets was not an issue on which they were willing to compromise.

The market areas of Georgian Dublin were far removed from the civility of the city's upper-class residential squares. Factional and gang violence, often with a strong sectarian edge, had been endemic in Dublin's markets since the 1720s. The 'Ormond Boys', for example, a Catholic gang that drew its strength from the meat markets in the north of the city earlier in the century, was known to sever the leg tendons of their enemies or leave unfortunate victims hanging by their jaws from meat hooks.[139] While such incidents were rare during the era of the Paving Board, the commissioners were still dealing with potentially dangerous and close-knit factions with strong territorial identities on a weekly basis.[140] The markets, as

---

136 Edel Sheridan, 'Designing the capital city' in Anngret Simms and Joseph Brady (eds), *Dublin through space and time* (Dublin, 2001), p. 79.
137 27 Jan. 1775 (PB/Mins/1, p. 176).
138 17 Mar. 1775 (PB/Mins/1, p. 206).
139 Maurice Craig, *Dublin 1660–1860* (Dublin, 2006), p. 114.
140 James Kelly, *The Liberty and Ormond boys* (Dublin, 2005), p. 22.

with many areas of the city, were also extremely filthy. This was brutally noted by Jonathan Swift in his poem *A description of a city shower* (London, 1710) where he described in graphic detail the flotsam brought onto the streets of an eighteenth-century city after a deluge:

> Now from all parts the swelling kennels flow,
> And bear their trophies with them as they go:
> Filth of all hues and odours seem to tell,
> What street they sailed from, by their sights and smell.
>
> ...
>
> Sweeping from butchers' stalls, dung, guts, and blood,
> Drowned puppies, stinking sprats, all drenched in mud,
> Dead cats, and turnip tops, come tumbling down the flood.

To the Paving Board, butchers' stall awnings fell under the classification applied to other structures of overhanging projections, as they reduced the available road space for carts and other vehicles. The butchers protested by pointing out that their awnings were necessary to protect their products from the sun and were thus vital to their business.[141] The matter came to a head in November 1775 when the commissioners decided to undertake a series of sweeping reforms of the markets decreeing that

> the corporation be empowered to remove all obstructions & nuisances in the several markets in the city ... of Dublin, & to oblige the tenants in possession of several stall in said markets, to affix their names, & number of the stalls they hold, under the penalty of ten shillings ... and to oblige all slaughterhouses & tallow chandler workshops, to be kept constantly beyond the city lamps, under heavy penalty.[142]

Several months later, however, the commissioners were still receiving complaints about bloody hides in Ormond Market and fruit stalls on Castle Street causing obstructions.[143] Nuisance inspectors were under strict instructions to ensure that each trader adhered to the Paving Board's rules, particularly the numbering of their

---

141 28 July 1775 (PB/Mins/1, p. 304).
142 3 Nov. 1775 (PB/Mins/1, p. 365).
143 5 Jan. 1776 (PB/Mins/1, p. 387).

stalls;[144] but the inspectors were quick to point out that, by working in a market area, they were not up against individuals but rather an entire community and would need significant constabulary assistance in order to complete their work.[145]

2.6   A late eighteenth-century cloth market similar to those encountered by the Paving Board (from Thomas Rowlandson, Rag Fair, Rosemary Lane, London (c.1800) (© The Trustees of the British Museum).

Despite the emphasis the Paving Board put on cleaning up many of Dublin's market areas, they did allow a special dispensation for markets on Plunket Street, near modern Francis Street:

> [This market] has been upwards of seventy years the only market or place for the sale of cloaths [*sic*] for the lower class of people, and that all houses and shops in the said street have pent-houses, shop-windows, and frames, which jet out into the said street, for the better exposing to sale the same cloth ... that no powers ... shall extend ... to the said street, as it will greatly injure the said market, and ruin the trade thereof, to the great prejudice and loss of a great number of industrious people.[146]

144   5 July 1780 (PB/Mins/7, p, 173).
145   17 July 1780 (PB/Mins/7, p. 193).
146   15 & 16 Geo. III, c. 20 [Ire.] (1775), clause xvi.

The city's sedan chairs also felt the impact of the Paving Board's regulations (Fig. 2.4). These chairs were a mode of human transport, similar to a palanquin, where an enclosed litter was carried by two or more footmen at the front and rear. They were a popular mode of travel for those that could afford them in eighteenth-century Europe. Capel Street was an area of the city that often encountered issues from sedan chairs parked so as to cause obstructions for other road users. Inspectors in that area were required to note the registration number of chairs being kept on footpaths and to inform their owners that if the behaviour continued that they would be fined.[147] The Capel Street sedans appear to have been slow in changing their ways, as they were still being reported the following year; however, they seem to have offered significantly less resistance than the city's butchers to the Paving Board's demands.[148]

Other forms of public transport were also encountered by the commissioners during the course of their duties. In October 1777, coach owner Thomas Murphy complained to the board that, while taking a fare along the Coombe at night, his horses fell into a hole in the road roughly five yards long, one yard wide and six feet deep. One of his horses had died at the scene, and he had little hope of the other recovering, and was thus seeking compensation of £19 from the Paving Board as the presence of this rather large obstacle fell under their remit.[149] That such large holes could exist in Dublin's streets seems somewhat difficult to believe, but it was not an isolated incident, with horses falling daily into a similar obstruction in Strand Street[150] and what was described as a 'chasm' opening up on High Street, making it

> impassable for several days past, to the great annoyance of the publick; the immediate danger of foot passengers; the detriment and injury of the industrious shop-keepers; and the stoppage of trade in one of the principal thoroughfares of this metropolis.[151]

Urban chasms were not the only worry for Dublin's equine residents, as noted in a message from the Paving Board to the dyers of the city

> that they will not be suffered to hang out cloths or silk or poles in the streets ... to desist from such practice, as these nuisances have been productive of very bad consequences, by frightening

---

147   17 Feb. 1775 (PB/Mins/1, p. 189).
148   23 Feb. 1776 (PB/Mins/2, p. 10).
149   10 Oct. 1777 (PB/Mins/3, p. 289).
150   *Dublin Journal*, 14 Sept. 1787.
151   *Freeman's Journal*, 29 Sept. 1774.

horses ridden or driven in the carriageways through the streets,
& prevent free circulation of air, so essential to the health of the
inhabitants.[152]

Despite rulings for the protection of horses on the city's streets, their owners were also the subject of several restricting guidelines. The Paving Board deemed it illegal to break, train or exercise horses, mares or geldings in Dublin's thoroughfares. Transgressors could be subject of fines of up to twenty shillings or the seizure of the animal in question due to the danger caused to the public.[153] Poor parking could also land a carriage owner in trouble with the Paving Board, as was discovered by Mr Michael Mills, whose car and horses were impounded for blocking a street, despite his protestations that 'it was only waiting while a cask of sugar which he bought was weighed'.[154]

Dublin's military community was another group that often fell victim to street hazards, although their incidences were regularly due to malicious behaviour rather than accident. During this period, Ireland had a large military presence owing to the geo-political manoeuvrings of the great European powers. While no other kingdom had a vested interest in Ireland as a possession, it was realised, particularly by the French who were keen to avenge their loss during the Seven Years War (1756–63), that by fermenting trouble on the island among the disenfranchised Catholics, important British military resources could be drained from other more globally important strategic theatres. As such, a large garrison was kept in the country during both peace and war time to deter foreign intervention and prevent revolt among the population. In addition to the barracked battalions consisting of several thousand men, there were up to 200 soldiers on duty in the city at any given time, with an entire company stationed at Dublin Castle and guards at Newgate Prison, the Tholsel and the Custom House.[155] A large group of men with regular pay, access to alcohol, weapons, no war to fight and often weak leadership due to the purchase system for officer commissions, frequently led to complaints of lack of discipline, drunkenness and general disobedience among the capital's soldiers.[156] Clashes, ranging from personal disputes, faction fighting and anti-imperialist sentiment, were frequent between soldiers and civilians through the era and across the country. In 1775, Lieutenant General Augustus Elliot (1717–90), commander-in-chief of armed forces in Ireland, wrote to the Paving Board complaining that soldiers returning along Barrack Street at night had been attacked

---

152   11 May 1781 (PB/Mins/8, p. 208).
153   25 Geo. III, c. 108 [Ire.] (1786).
154   1 Nov. 1785 (PB/Mins/16, p. 204).
155   McBride, *Eighteenth-century Ireland*, p. 42.
156   Ibid., p. 40.

and that stalls, bulks, pillars & sheds in said street, affording shelter & lurking places for the persons who have been guilty of said offences, & also opportunity to escape being brought to justice, has been in some measure a cause there of.[157]

Attacks on soldiers around this period had been growing in frequency, with Dublin Corporation expressing their 'abhorrence of the cruel treatment ... the soldiers quartered in this city have received from certain wicked and ill-disposed persons.'[158] It must be noted that the soldiers did little to enamour the public to them through unsanctioned reprisals,[159] and with the growing escalation of the American Revolutionary War (1775–83) and political discord with Britain, relations between soldiers, Dubliners and the Paving Board grew worse over the 1770s and 1780s.[160]

One strata of society that the commissioners were particularly skilled at dealing with was the powerful or wealthy residents of the city who felt that rules could be bent or altered to suit them. A prime example can be found in a carefully worded letter from the Paving Board to the Archbishop of Dublin regarding the lack of pavement in front of his stables on Merrion Square. The Archbishop was unhappy about receiving a complaint from the third division supervisor; however, as the central board replied,

> this board never intended to treat him with any disrespect, & to represent that every person, nobility as well as gentry, are obliged to pave before coach houses & stables at their own expense, exclusive of the paving tax on their houses ... his Grace cannot be a stranger to the general complaint of the bad condition of the streets, & unless every person comply, it is impossible to have them in proper repair.[161]

---

157 31 Mar. 1775 (PB/Mins/1, p. 221).
158 4 Feb. 1775; Gilbert (ed.), *Calendar of ancient records*, xii, p. 347.
159 Ibid.; Kelly, *The Liberty and Ormond boys*, p. 22.
160 19 Oct. 1784 (PB/Mins/13, p. 76); 3 Dec. 1784 (PB/Mins/13, p. 176).
161 3 Dec. 1779 (PB/Mins/6, p. 243).

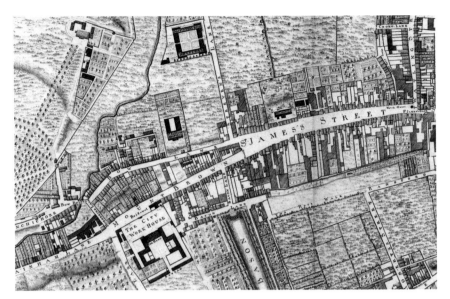

2.7   The St. James' Gate area just prior to the founding of the Guinness Brewery in 1759
(from John Rocque, An exact survey of the city of Dublin (1756), courtesy of the
Board of Trinity College Dublin).

The commissioners' work also brought them into contact with one of Dublin's
better-known businessmen from the era: Arthur Guinness (1725–1803). The
Guinness brewery was founded in 1759 at St James' Gate in the west of the city
under a 9,000 year lease (Fig. 2.7). By the late 1760s, the establishment was already
producing large quantities of stout and Guinness was noted as a brewer of great
reputation and one of the city's leading industrialists.

Unfortunately he was no stranger to service providers like the Paving Board
intruding on his business. In 1775, he had become involved with a bitter dispute
with Dublin Corporation regarding access to vital water supplies for his St
James' Gate site. The corporation intended to fill in a water course on city land
that Guinness and others were technically not entitled to use. During the course
of tense negotiations over the issue, Guinness informed the corporation that he
would defend his water access 'through force of arms' if necessary and taunted
them 'to try how far their strength would prevail'.[162] Refusing to be intimidated,
the corporation proceeded with their work under the protection of the local sheriff
and his two assistants. On reaching the site, the work party was initially obstructed
by one of Guinness' employees who was swiftly removed by the sheriff. Events
became more heated when Guinness himself arrived:

---

162   4 Feb. 1775; Gilbert (ed.), *Calendar of ancient records*, xii, p. 365.

[he] violently rushed upon them wrenching a pickaxe from one [labourer] and declaring with very much improper language, that they should not proceed. [The PWC's] committee expostulated on this impropriety of conduct, but he remained obstinate, and when the labourers were ordered to proceed, stood with the pickaxe in the way and prevented them, and declared that if they filled [the water course] up from end to end he would immediately open it.

The standoff eventually ended when Guinness promised to file an official request for access with the PWC, which he promptly failed to do, instead serving the corporation with an injunction to maintain his water source.

In 1781, the Paving Board found that it was necessary to widen St James' Gate, the site of a former medieval gatehouse that was part of the city's defensive perimeter. According to the Paving Board's plans, this street widening would unfortunately require the partial demolition of the Guinness brewery. Guinness, in the wake of his previous difficult dealings with the corporation, was highly vocal in defending his property, informing the board

> that whenever this work is doing it will ... stop his brewing business, as a great part of the brewery will be to be removed in consequence, which will make it tedious, & it will therefore require great previous preparation to avoid the total ruin of his trade.[163]

In this case, the dramatic scenes of 1775 were thankfully avoided and, fortunately for generations of Dubliners and stout drinkers worldwide, the commissioners' work at St James' Gate did not unduly damage Guinness' business. The brewery is still in operation at the same site to the present day.

Paving

Despite the attention the Paving Board gave to dealing with complaints and issues from Dublin's different industries and communities, its primary concern still focused on laying and maintaining the city's pavements and streets. Determining which of Dublin's labyrinth of thoroughfares across its jurisdiction would be dealt with as a significant priority, the commissioners worked to the following guideline: 'that a street not at all paved, is in a worse state than a street that hath

---

163   23 June 1781 (PB/Mins/8, p. 265).

2.8   Saint Catherine's, Thomas Street, Dublin by James Malton (1792). Ink and watercolour
       (53.3 x 77.4cm). Thomas Street was one of the primary thoroughfares in the fifth
       division (NGI 2186; photograph courtesy of the National Gallery of Ireland ©).

Owen was not the only surveyor working on Dublin's pavements during this
time. Residents of Grafton Street approached the commissioners in 1775 to
complain that a new level of pavement and flagging on their street would cause
them great inconvenience and they had an alternative plan that they would like
to submit. The author of this plan was Owen's former rival William Cox, who
had been hired directly by the residents.[187] The commissioners sided with Owen's
original plan; however, they may have been impressed with the quality of Cox's
work as he was occasionally used to produce surveys directly for the Paving Board
after this event.[188] Assistant city surveyor David Worthington also dealt with the
commissioners during their early years, albeit relatively rarely, and primarily about
their jurisdiction boundaries.[189] Like Owen, little is known about Worthington.
He began work with Dublin Corporation in the 1770s as an assistant to Thomas
Mathews and was eventually appointed to the position of city surveyor in 1795
at the death of his predecessor, Samuel Byron.[190] Unfortunately he only held the
position for just over six years before passing away in 1801.[191]

187   12 May 1775 (PB/Mins/1, p. 255).
188   22 Sept. 1775 (PB/Mins/1, p. 341).
189   30 Jan. 1778 (PB/Mins/4, p. 38).
190   *Dublin Evening Post*, 8 Sept. 1795.
191   1801; Gilbert (ed.), *Calendar of ancient records*, xv, p. 216.

The Pipe Water Committee

One public body that the commissioners of the Paving Board had regular and often difficult relations with was the Pipe Water Committee (PWC). This organisation, run solely by members of Dublin Corporation, was responsible for water supply and taxing Dublin's citizens for their water. This was an increasingly important organisation as Dublin's more progressive and expanding neighbourhoods sought their own personal supply of water from the city's reservoirs, rather than having to resort to a communal well, pump or open water source.[192] The primary cause of conflict between the two organisations originated in a lack of a coherent cooperative strategy between them: the Paving Board wanted to lay pavement while the PWC wanted to dig it up and both appear to have worked (for the most part) independently from each other.

Underground water pipes during the late eighteenth-century were made of wood and thus had to be replaced every ten to fourteen years to prevent them from rotting completely.[193] To ensure that pipes were regularly replaced and that houses were connected to the supply lines, the PWC was empowered to dig up pavement but was often 'guilty of neglects in repairing the same.'[194] To avoid the Paving Board having to pay to pave a street twice, in theory, any pavement laid down after water pipe works would be financed by the residences that had requested the PWC's attention.[195]

This disparity could lead to great confusion, particularly from the ordinary residents of the city. In 1776 the inhabitants of Granby Row and Henry Street informed the Paving Board that their streets had originally been well paved but had been recently pulled up and 'rendered almost impassable' due to pipe works,[196] while the next year the residents of Mary Street took the proactive step of writing to the commissioners, asking them to delay their work as water pipes were in the process of being laid.[197] Paving Board supervisors were under direct orders not to allow residents to break up paving so that they could install piping themselves unless that had 'proper authority from the person appointed by the corporation for the city of Dublin to superintend the same'.[198] When the PWC dug up and repaired streets, the Paving Board often found their results to be 'in a very improper & imperfect

---

192   William Curry, *The picture of Dublin: or, stranger's guide to the Irish metropolis* (Dublin, 1835), p. 100.
193   LaTouche, et al., *Report of the commissioners*, p. 6.
194   18 Oct. 1777 (PB/Mins/3, p. 292).
195   15 & 16 Geo. III, c. 20 [Ire.] (1775), clause xxii.
196   22 Mar. 1776 (PB/Mins/2, p. 42).
197   20 June 1777 (PB/Mins/3, p. 166).
198   25 Apr. 1777 (PB/Mins/3, p. 90).

manner',[199] despite the board's insistence that any pipe water works should 'always be done with as little detriment and inconvenience' to the public as possible.[200] This issue left ordinary Dubliners with a significant problem – they could either have pipes laid by the PWC but then have poor-quality paving, or have high-quality paving but then go to the expense of getting permission to open the paths to lay their own pipes. When questioned on the matter, Owen felt that if proper regulations were set up between the two bodies they could function adequately in tandem, but as the Paving Board's surveyor he was well aware of the problems the PWC were causing in the streets:

> There certainly have been a great many complaints made of the proceedings of the PWC to the Paving Board; it is impossible where the pavement is broke up by the [PWC] that it can often be made as good as before the street is broke up.[201]

Eventually the commissioners issued a notice to the residents of Dublin to try and regulate the often conflicting process:

> [When a pipe water main is being laid] that by a late act of parliament every person is to pay for the pipe water, whether they have a pipe or not; if you intend to fix a branch to the new main, you are to do it while the ground is open, & if you neglect to take that opportunity, you will not be permitted to break up the street after it is paved.[202]

These clashing projects are an interesting example of the civic minefield that Dubliners had to traverse in order to see their city improved, with bodies such as the WSC, Ballast Board, PWC and, of course, the Paving Board, working separately until the Dublin Improvement Act (1849) brought many of their responsibilities under the control of the city's corporation. Until that time however, Dublin had to make do with the organisations it had.

Scavengers

Waste removal is a vital part of any large urban community. It prevents the spread of disease, reduces the presence of vermin and adds greatly to the pleasantness of any town or city. Household waste in the eighteenth century was primarily organic,

---

199   18 Oct. 1777 (PB/Mins/3, p. 292); 3 Apr. 1778 (PB/Mins/4, p. 98).
200   15 & 16 Geo. III, c. 20 [Ire.] (1775), clause xxvii.
201   Evidence of Thomas Owen; Blaquiere report (1784), quoted in LaTouche, et al., *Report of the commissioners*, p. 283.
202   25 July 1778 (PB/Mins/4, p. 265).

consisting of food, human and animal waste, coal-ash or the debris of household maintenance and was nearly all recyclable due to the lack of modern synthetic materials. This is an important point to note as waste removal contractors, known at the time as *scavengers*, had a continual stream of profitable recyclable material without the necessity to resort to landfill. The term 'scavenger', while seeming harsh, is apt as these individuals were responsible for sorting waste into its separate aggregates such as manure, ash, cloth, wood or metal, all of which could be sold for profit. It was estimated at the time that a good scavenger crew could fill and tip up to eight cart loads of waste a day.[203]

The role that waste removal played in Dublin's infrastructure during this era is evident in John Rocque's *An exact survey of the city and suburbs of Dublin* (Dublin, 1756) John Rocque (*c*.1709–62) was a land surveyor and cartographer of French Huguenot descent. Raised in London, he followed his older brother Bartholomew into designing and laying out decorative gardens for stately homes before progressing onto land surveying and map production. Known for his use of highly accurate trigonometric surveys and accomplished copper-plate engraving techniques, Rocque produced an acclaimed map of London in twenty-four parts in 1747. His cartographic style was noted for its realism and artistic flair and by the 1750s he was at work producing his celebrated *An exact survey of Dublin*. This map far outclassed traditional Irish urban surveying in its style, detail and accuracy and is still regarded as one of the most important and recognisable pieces of pre-Ordinance Survey mapping of the city. Aside from his cartographic legacy Rocque made a significant impact in the Irish survey industry through his French School of disciples. These surveyors, including Bernard Scalé (1739–1829), Thomas Sherrard (1750–1837) and William Longfield (1825–*c*.1870), stretched over several professional generations and retained Rocque's flair for business, art and professionalism.[204] During the course of his highly detailed mapping exercise for Dublin, Rocque took the time and effort to note and include dunghills scattered throughout the outskirts of the city. They were physically part of the urban landscape. Waste removal was so important that Rocque even included a topographical representation of what appears to be the city's largest dump on the appropriately named Dunghill Lane near Usher's Quay (Fig. 2.9).[205] Unlike the modern world, waste storage facilities such as Dublin's various dunghills were highly visible and often located close to or in the environment in which the waste was gathered. The location of any dump in an urban environment, particularly

---

203   Evidence of John Price King; Blaquiere report (1784), quoted in LaTouche, et al., *Report of the commissioners*, p. 229.
204   Ó Cionnaith, *Mapping, measurement and metropolis*, pp 17–19, 156–67.
205   Modern day Island Street.

for animal or human waste (subtly referred to as 'night soil' in the Paving Board minute books) was bound to draw protest from local residents. The inhabitants of New Street South once wrote to the Paving Board in 1779 to complain

> That their neighbourhood is greatly annoyed by scavengers, throwing their dirt at the corner of the Long Lane [and] New Street ... & together with the very offensive smell is exceedingly injurious and unwholesome; that they are informed the owners of the ground or dunghills, were served with notice to enclose the same, which they pay no regard to.[206]

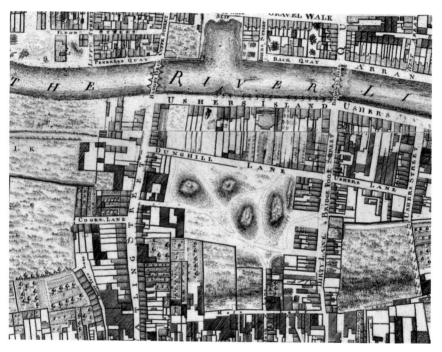

2.9   Dunghill Lane near Thomas Street and its piles of waste (centre) demonstrated the impact scavengers had on the city (from John Rocque, *An exact survey of the city of Dublin* (1756), courtesy of the Board of Trinity College Dublin).

Large animals had a far greater presence in the city than they currently do as cattle, sheep and pigs could only be slaughtered close to market due to the lack of refrigeration. This meant that the general public had far greater exposure to their waste. Free-roaming pigs were noted by the Paving Board as being a particular problem in Dublin during this time, with the board authorizing any member of the public to 'seize, kill, or carry away the same ... for his or her own use' when one was spotted.[207] Run-off from slaughterhouses and markets, coupled with

---

206   11 June 1779 (PB/Mins/6, p. 46).
207   25 Geo. III, c. 108 [Ire.] (1786).

thousands of horses, mules and donkeys, plus the presence of ash from household fires and overall general domestic and industrial refuse, meant that the role of a scavenger was most necessary in keeping Dublin clean, functioning and, given the era, relatively healthy.

The city's scavengers were hired directly by the lord mayor on a contractual basis but placed under the supervision of the Paving Board who monitored their work. Scavengers were responsible for collecting, removing and disposing of street waste within the city suburbs with the Paving Board division supervisors monitoring their effectiveness.[208] The commissioners spent on average around £1,000 per year for this service and their comments about contractors and scavenging work were noted regularly in board meetings.[209]

Like all large metropolitan areas, not all Dublin citizens were as careful doing their share to keep the city's streets clean and the nuisance inspectors were kept busy reporting residents that did not comply with the Paving Board's waste rules. Each resident within the Paving Board's jurisdiction was required to sweep and clean the footway in front of their house before 8am between May and September and before 10am between October and April.[210] Fines could be issued for leaving waste in front of houses outside of designated hours, neglecting to sweep the pavement, placing coal-ash on the footway,[211] or for fly-tipping, which was noted as being a significant problem, albeit for political reasons, at the equestrian statue of King William III in College Green.[212]

Residents of the poorer areas of the city, particularly in the fifth, sixth and seventh divisions, had a more difficult time in disposing of their waste due to a lack of amenities. This left them at a higher risk of being fined by the Paving Board, and as one division inspector noted, this situation was highly unfair:

> There are many thousands of poor-room-keepers in Dublin, who have no place whatsoever in which to deposit filth, except the streets, which is one principal cause of increasing the labour of the scavengers, besides being an offensive nuisance; persons offending as above have often been brought before the Board

---

208   3 Nov. 1775 (PB/Mins/1, p. 366).
209   6 Sept. 1782 (PB/Mins/10, p. 24).
210   15 & 16 Geo. III, c. 20 [Ire.] (1775), clauses xxvi.
211   22 Aug. 77 (PB/Mins/3, p. 271).
212   6 Sept. 1782 (PB/Mins/10, p. 31).

and fined; but [the inspector] considers this a great hardship on the individuals, in punishment for what they cannot help, and in extracting a fine, which they are unable to pay.[213]

If the Paving Board had been more proactive in trying to assist or prevent the dumping of waste in public streets, its efforts may have been best directed towards providing adequate waste facilities. However, with its limited resources and mandate, it was restricted to simply trying to remove the waste as best as possible rather than implementing a long-term and sustainable waste-management plan for the city. It tackled the symptoms rather than finding a long-term solution. It was noted at the time that many of the larger markets, dairies and slaughterhouses found within the city were without sewers 'or any other means of preserving cleanliness, in consequence of which the filth is accumulated in the most noxious and offensive manner'.[214] This in turn could pollute the entire neighbouring area as well as requiring the increased attention (and cost) of scavengers to remove waste that could have been dealt with by sewers. Owen felt that this problem could be remedied if all major streets were provided with a central sewer, but with the Paving Board lacking funds, his proposal that such works should be sponsored directly by heavily taxed local residents may not have been prudent.[215]

Scavengers had other duties aside from waste removal. Heavy and prolonged snow falls are infrequent in Dublin, but when they do occur they can cause havoc. During such periods of inclement weather the city's scavengers were called upon to help open the streets to pedestrians and traffic by clearing snow. To assist them, each residence was responsible for sweeping snow from in front of their house with those that did not cooperate being fined by the Paving Board.[216] Scavengers also played the important role of making sure that grates and sewer openings were clear so as to allow melting snow to run-off freely:

> The directors and commissioners for Paving ... acquaints the public, that to prevent as far as possible, inconvenience by the very sudden thaw, they have ordered the scavengers to clear the channels of the streets ... and they request the inhabitants will be particular in instructing their servants to scrape the snow carefully from the footways, and also to assist in clearing the channels, as

---

213 Evidence of Thomas Lyness; quoted in LaTouche, et al., *Report of the commissioners*, p. 8.
214 Ibid.
215 Evidence of Thomas Owen; Blaquiere report (1784), quoted in LaTouche, et al., *Report of the commissioners*, p. 283.
216 *Dublin Journal*, 21 Dec. 1786.

they fear from the great extent of the city, it will be otherwise impossible to put the streets into that immediate order for the public accommodation that they would wish.[217]

Despite their vital role in Dublin's infrastructure, scavengers could at times cause the commissioners significant issues. As unregulated contractors to the city, they were under continuous pressure to keep their costs as low as possible to increase their profit margins. This pressure often led to a poor quality of service and regularly led them into direct conflict with the Paving Board. If a local inspector found that waste had not been removed from a particular street, he would hire an additional scavenger cart, referred to at the time as a 'sweeper', to clean up after the contractor. The contractor would then be fined for leaving waste uncollected and for the price of the sweeper. This was the difficult situation that John Price King, supervisor of the first division, found himself in during the early 1780s (see Fig. 2.10). King was responsible for inspecting the scavengers' work and making sure that the streets had been cleaned adequately. In the winter of 1782 he was forced to employ a number of sweeper carts as the local scavenger crews had not fully performed their duties. The scavengers were greatly upset that their work was being criticised, that outsiders had been brought into their territory and that their job security was under threat. When an appeal to the board was rejected they resorted to intimidation and force to get their way. While loading sweeper carts on Church Street, an aggrieved scavenger, John McCabe, attacked a sweeper cart and

> threw the dirt out of one of his carts, saying, he had cleansed the street on Friday, and that [King] had no right to cleanse it on the Monday following; and in a part of Smithfield, where there was a heap of dirt, prevented his men from taking away the dirt by force.[218]

217 *Dublin Journal*, 3 Jan. 1786.
218 Evidence of John Price King; Blaquiere report (1784), quoted in LaTouche, et al., *Report of the commissioners*, p. 229.

2.10   The first division witnessed increased disputes between the Paving Board and
        scavengers during the 1780s (from John Rocque, *An exact survey of the city of Dublin*
        (1756), courtesy of the Board of Trinity College Dublin).

The scavenger situation only grew worse in the first division as the resentment from
contracted crews grew towards King's supervision. A sweeper cart was blocked in
on Henrietta Street by larger scavenger carts and the sweeper, once he managed to
escape, was followed and harassed by the scavengers along the rest of his route.[219]
Passions were so high during this event that one scavenger was heard to exclaim
'he would lose his life rather than suffer [the sweeper] to take away one pound of
dirt'.[220] The levels of violence from scavengers increased as the year progressed. On
another occasion a scavenger attempted to force a sweeper horse and cart off the
quays and into the Liffey,[221] while in the fifth division a sweeper was ambushed
during the course of his duties:

219   Ibid.
220   Ibid.
221   Evidence of Owen Caffrey; ibid., p. 230.

He was prevented by one William Johnston, who is son to George Johnston, scavenger, who seized the horses by the head, and would not let him go to the place where the dirt was. Witness then took the horse by the heads, upon which Johnston swore a great oath that he would throw him down and trample upon him.[222]

All the Paving Board could do in such situations was protest or complain to the lord mayor about his contractors. Scavengers were not employees of the Paving Board and so while it was officially responsible for cleaning Dublin's streets, it had no authority over the men doing the work outside of supervision and fines. While waste removal in Dublin ran relatively well by eighteenth-century standards, there were times when the situation grew so bad that the Paving Board resorted to offering 5 shillings to anyone who would remove 'dirt or filth' per cartload, which they were willing to supply.[223] One division supervisor lamented that 'Many of those heaps of filth have been accumulating for years; the stench is always offensive, but especially during the summer months'.[224] Like other aspects of maintaining Dublin's streets, coordinating scavenger crews was often a difficult, arduous and highly visible task that could result in unwanted attention directed towards the Paving Board. Yet, like paving, the Paving Board's main success with scavenging lay in how it managed to centralise a divergent and scattered city service under one central authority.

The dangers of Dublin's streets

Issues surrounding verbal and physical assaults were not limited to scavengers. Supervisors, inspectors and collectors often felt the full brunt of public resentment against the board's intrusion on people's lives and these encounters, scattered throughout the board's minute books, provide vivid details of the relationship that the Paving Board had with sections of the public.

Assaults on Paving Board staff during the early years of the body were primarily related to two main areas of conflict: taxation and territory. Resentment to taxation is an understandable and relatable aspect of human civilisation throughout time. Collectors were required to visit every house within their division to collect a specific figure based on the value of the property. This face-to-face interaction proved dangerous for Paving Board staff, such as when one tax collector was physically thrown out of the house of Henry Carlson of Kirwan Street, who

---

222   Evidence of William Kennedy; ibid., p. 231.
223   24 Nov. 1780 (PB/Mins/8, p. 25).
224   Evidence of Thomas Lyness; quoted in LaTouche, et al., *Report of the commissioners*, p. 8.

had been avoiding paying his dues. This was made all the worse by the fact that the collector had been accompanied by a parish constable, who had also been physically ejected by Carlson.[225] A mirror-opposite incident occurred several weeks later when a collector paid a visit to Nicholas Merrick of Patrick Street, a similar tax dodger. Upon entering Merrick's home, the collector was violently assaulted and held hostage until his eventual release thanks to the actions of a constable.[226] With no independent citywide police force, the parochial nature of many of these tax disputes occasionally meant that constables and watchmen, appointed on a parish-by-parish basis, were often reluctant to become involved or to come to the assistance of Paving Board employees that were attacked by local residents.

Despite having the legal backing of the Paving Board it appears that the collectors were not a group who would accept such abuse without proper compensation and were willing to organise among themselves for better working conditions. In 1776, a memorial from the collectors of each division was read to the Paving Board informing the board of the excellent work they had collectively done for which they 'received great abuse & insult' from the general public.[227] The collectors felt that their cut of the tax received was insufficient given the dangers they faced and requested that they instead be granted a commission of one shilling per pound they collected. This was eventually approved by the board.

As perilous as the work of a collector could be, most of the more serious recorded assaults took place due to the issue of territory or ownership. Staff encroaching on citizens' neighbourhoods, homes, possessions or daily lives during the course of their duties could spark spontaneous acts of violence and resistance against the Paving Board from both individuals and mobs. The act of parliament that had created the Paving Board had anticipated the possibility of such assaults and in one of its many clauses a note was made that

> [anyone who] hereafter obstructs, hinders, or molests [an officer] in the performance or execution of their duty ... shall for the first offence forfeit the sum of twenty shillings, for the second offence the sum of forty shillings, for the third and every other offence the sum of three pounds; and in the case of non-payment be sent to the house of correction for one month.[228]

---

225 10 Mar. 1780 (PB/Mins/6, p. 21).
226 8 Apr. 1780 (PB/Mins/6, p. 52).
227 24 May 1776 (PB/Mins/1, p. 120).
228 15 & 16 Geo. III, c. 20 [Ire.] (1775), clauses xxx.

For example fines of up to 20 shillings were levied against the assailants of a Paving Board officer who was assaulted on North Anne Street for trying to prevent the stealing of pavement slabs,[229] and against wheelwright Michael Fail of New Street South who set upon Paving Board employee Thomas Jackson while he was dispensing public notices.[230] Fines, no matter how steep, could only act as a deterrent and for the most part staff were on their own in dealing with the public during their normal duties.

One of the more serious incidents relating to property occurred in October 1777. The inspector of nuisances in the second division, Thomas Barker, reported the owner of a public house on Capel Street, Mr Phipps, as blocking the footpath and carriageway with empty casks. This was an obvious violation of the Paving Board's rules and therefore Barker was empowered to confiscate the offending casks. Phipps took offence to his property being confiscated, gathered a number of men and forcibly took the casks from Barker, who was beaten to the floor and set upon by a mob that 'called him the worst names'. When the incident was reported to the commissioners they fined Phipps five shillings for obstructing Capel Street with his casks and twenty shillings for 'obstructing, hindering & molesting' Barker. A month later Phipps was still refusing to pay and was strongly reminded that

> the Act of Parliament [for paving] orders & directs in case of non payment of fines for such offences, the person or persons offending, to be sent to the house of correction for one month, and that this board is determined to enforce obedience to its orders.[231]

Point made, Phipps eventually paid in early December, narrowly missing out on a month in prison. However, Capel Street would prove to be an increasingly dangerous area for Paving Board staff during the 1780s (see p. 96). The commissioners also appear to have been aware that the power of their organisation could be used against their wishes at street level by corrupt employees. In 1781 they issued a decree stating that any property seized by their officers, such as in the Phipps case, could not be sold on for profit by the staff member on pain of suspension.[232]

After eight years of work throughout the city, storm clouds began to gather on the Paving Board's horizons. Rumours of abuse of power, not from its inspectors but from the upper echelons of the organisation, would prove to be a major issue

229   26 Jan. 1778 (PB/Mins/4, p. 221).
230   25 July 1778 (PB/Mins/4, p. 265).
231   21 Nov. 1777 (PB/Mins/3, p. 344).
232   21 Sept. 1781 (PB/Mins/9, p. 64).

a man of the purest intention and greatest public spirit and one who would think it no honour to be named in a commission from which the rest of his fellow citizens were so unjustly and so disgracefully excluded.[246]

While such debates on the future of the Paving Board raged in parliament, work continued on improving Dublin's streets, albeit understandably with less vigour than before. There was a notable reduction in projects undertaken by the interim commissioners throughout the rest of spring and early summer of 1782, which under normal circumstances would have been one of their peak construction periods of the year. There was also a prominent decrease in the number of references made to Owen's work during the same period, with only four surveys recorded from March to July of that year.[247] Fortunately for him the interim commission was in place only to keep the lights burning until a suitable long-term arrangement could be reached.

The new parliamentary paving act came into effect in August 1782[248] with the founding of the second Dublin Paving Board at the Dublin Society House, Grafton Street. This newly constituted board, made up of a similar number of representatives as the first board, attacked its duties with notable energy, represented by a distinguishable increase in focus in their minute books. New elections were held for commissioners with ten members per division, the majority of whom were new to the work of the Paving Board, including MPs Luke Gardiner (1745–98) and Sir Boyle Roche (1736–1807), while some level of association with Dublin Corporation remained through the involvement of several aldermen.[249] Existing officers from the body's previous incarnation were retained, including long-term clerk Richard Gladwell, who was asked to present a report on projects current underway, and Owen, 'the surveyor of the late corporation', who presented a review of work required in each division.[250] His evaluation showed that at the time repairs were taking place on North King Street, Dawson Street, Bridgefoot Street and Essex Quay, while work was required on Bolton Street and Dorset Street. For the meantime Owen was to continue his role and supervise these projects; however, his position would not remain secure for long.

---

246   Ibid.
247   30 Mar. 1782; 5 Apr. 1782; 28 June 1782; 20 July 1782 (PB/Mins/9, pp 261, 271, 352, 343).
248   21 & 22 Geo. III, c. 60 [Ire.] (1782).
249   7 Aug. 1782 (PB/Mins/10, pp 1–6); see appendix for list of elected commissioners to the second Paving Board.
250   7 Aug. 1782 (PB/Mins/10, p. 3).

Owen's young challenger

A short notice in the *Dublin Gazette* to appoint officers to the board was published several weeks after the new commissioners first met. The advertised positions included treasurer, clerk, inspector of received accounts, divisional receivers and surveyor. An internal memo at the time also requested each division not to elect anyone they suspected of selling 'malt or spirituous liqueurs' which they felt may clash with their official duties as representatives of the board.[251] Owen was now faced with the prospect of having to compete for his own job and be judged proficient by a group of men who had made clear, at least at face value, that they were eager to see significant changes within the organisation.

There were two contenders for the advertised role of surveyor, Owen and Arthur Richard Neville. Neville was only beginning his career as a surveyor in 1782, but his family had a significant history within the industry. The Nevilles were land surveyors akin to the likes of John Rocque or Owen's previous opponents William Cox and Thomas Mathews. Arthur's father, Jacob, had attempted to produce a map of County Wicklow between 1752 and 1754; however, he ran into significant financial difficulties from the start of this ambitious project with the final map not appearing until six years later.[252] During the same period he also authored a treatise in land surveying 'showing everything useful in the art of surveying'[253] and by the 1770s had moved to Dublin and was operating a successful private business. Sons following in their fathers' businesses were relatively common in the surveying industry during this period,[254] and Arthur was more than ready to reference his father's prestige to assist his own advancement, as shown by his application to the Paving Board:

> he was educated in his business under his father, who was very
> eminent: & has had ten years practice, which has matured his
> knowledge & referring to a recommendation signed by several
> noblemen & gentlemen, praying to be appointed surveyor, & if
> appointed, he hopes to perform the duties to general satisfaction.[255]

Hints to Neville's young age are alluded to in the above memorial. The word 'matured' stands out, with his ten year's experience probably being served as apprentice to his father from around the age of fourteen. Neville is also known to have died around 1830, almost forty years after Owen did and almost half a century

---

251 12 Aug. 1782 (PB/Mins/10, p. 6).
252 *Dublin Journal*, 14. Mar. 1761.
253 J.H. Andrews, *Plantation acres* (Omagh, 1985), p. 431.
254 O'Cionnaith, *Mapping, measurement and metropolis*, pp 17–19.
255 28 Aug. 1782 (PB/Mins/10, p. 23).

after applying to work for the Paving Board , thus reinforcing the assumption that he was probably in his early twenties at the start of the second Paving Board and perhaps slightly too young for the commissioners' liking.

Owen came into the competition with a distinct advantage as he had, apart from a few minor complaints, fulfilled the role adequately since 1774.

> A memorial of Thomas Owen was read, setting forth that having [performed] the difficult & arduous task or employment of surveyor for upwards of eight years, which he hopes is considered as having filled with ability & integrity: He is emboldened to request the favour and patronage of the board to be re-elected, which he will endeavour to merit by a strict attention to his duty.[256]

The competition was one-sided and Owen was elected unanimously by the new commissioners. This defeat was only a temporary setback for Neville. During the 1790s he worked as an assistant to the Dublin city surveyor Samuel Byron, who was noted for his exceptional artistic skills when producing maps, including a 'universally approved' plan of the ornamental grounds in Merrion Square.[257] Arthur was admitted as a freeman to the city of Dublin in 1795,[258] following in the footsteps of his grandfather who received the honour back in 1704,[259] and was eventually elected to the role of city surveyor for the corporation in 1801. He held the position until 1828 when it was passed to his son, Arthur Jr, until the post was discontinued in the 1850s.[260]

Taking stock of Dublin's streets

With their new regime now in place, the second Paving Board could commence its work in earnest. One of its more pressing issues was an adequate financial strategy to allow it to maintain the city's streets for the years to come. It had, however, many substantial obstacles to overcome to achieve this goal. The act of parliament that created the second board was highly critical of the expenditure versus results of the first incarnation of the Paving Board:

---

256 Ibid.
257 *Dublin Chronicle*, 31 July 1788.
258 16 Jan. 1795; Gilbert (ed.), *Calendar of ancient records*, xiv, p. 398.
259 Mary Clark, *The book of maps of the Dublin city surveyors, 1695–1827* (Dublin, 1983), p. xv.
260 Ibid., p. xvii.

A considerable debt still remains due by the corporation constituted by the said acts, on account of the execution thereof, and many streets and other places are in a worse condition then they were before ... and the benefits to the publick expected to arise thereby, have not occurred.

On top of this central financial issue the new commissioners found that the seventh division in the south of the city (Fig. 3.1) was of significant economic concern. The commissioners agreed that even if all outstanding taxes due in that division were collected, the amount would still fall considerably short of what was required. This problem was exacerbated as the income levels of the residents of the seventh division were very low.[261]

3.1   The seventh division in the south of the city repeatedly ran into financial problems (from John Rocque, *An exact survey of the city of Dublin* (1756), courtesy of the Board of Trinity College Dublin).

261   28 Oct. 1782 (PB/Mins/10, p. 96).

Despite such fiscal burdens, work had to continue. Street repairs in the Coombe and Francis Street[262] were among some of the first works conducted by the second Paving Board, as well as works in Smithfield, with street conditions reported as being 'so extremely bad, that it is not passable on horseback, & at night there is a great danger in walking there'.[263] The minute books of the Paving Board also represent a significant change in attitude towards work in the organisation. Records were shorter and snappier than those prior to 1782 and overall the body appeared to have approached its duties with more energy and professionalism than existed in the final days of the first board. The second Paving Board was also increasingly active in calling on Owen's opinion concerning the materials it used. In December 1782 he was asked to undertake a review of an urban stone yard near Gardiner Street, 'as far as he is able, to distinguish the quantity of inferior stones & gravel'.[264] He was also to identify the amount of material that had been removed by the first Paving Board from the same yard and to calculate the value of its worth based on his volumetric analysis.

During the early months of 1783 Owen was kept extremely busy trying to satisfy the new commissioners' desire for as much information as possible on the state of Dublin's streets. Key to this was a request to create a detailed thematic list of the state of repair of streets in each division; in essence a city-wide stocktaking exercise. This was a substantial surveying project to undertake and pushed Owen's resources to their absolute limit. Despite delving into the work and having the confidence of the new board, he soon found himself under growing pressure from it to complete his assigned task that was key to its strategic plan. Evidence of how hectic his duties were during this period can be seen in a complaint from the plumber of Dublin Corporation, who said that he was having huge difficulties in tracking down Owen, even finding him absent from his home, as Owen's approval was needed to issue licences to legally open up paving.[265] In March of that year Owen reported

> that he finds the return the board ordered him to make of the measurement &c. of the several streets, is much more difficult than he apprehended ... that the severity of the weather, together with the other business of the corporation has prevented him being ready so soon as he expected, but he thinks the whole will be finished the first week of May.[266]

262 27 Sept. 1782 (PB/Mins/10, p. 62).
263 29 Aug. 1783 (PB/Mins/11, p. 36).
264 13 Dec. 1782 (PB/Mins/10, p. 156).
265 14 Feb. 1783 (PB/Mins/10, p. 184).
266 28 Mar. 1783 (PB/Mins/10, p. 233).

May passed, then June. In keeping with the duchess of Leinster's opinion of Owen's tardiness, his results, despite being very detailed and precise, were not laid before the board until mid-September. Owen had measured almost every street, lane, market and alley in the city. He had systematically divided each thoroughfare into one of three categories: greatest wear, less wear and least wear. Of the measured streets, 45 per cent were considered to have the greatest level of wear, 25 per cent were noted as requiring maintenance (but not urgently) and the remainder were of little or no concern.[267] When Owen's figures are analysed proportionally to the area of each division, a striking picture of the quality of Dublin's streets is presented. In the third division alone, covering much of the south-east of the city, just over 70 per cent of streets were considered as poor quality, followed closely by the sixth division at 66 per cent and the fourth division at 64 per cent. Of the main streets requiring repair, it was estimated that Great Britain Street (modern Parnell Street) would cost £2,000, Capel Street at £1,800, while Mary, Henry and Grafton Streets would cost around £2,500.

This project perhaps best sums up the importance of the role of quantitative and spatial measurement performed by the surveyor of the Paving Board. Owen's spatial and technical analysis quantified, qualified and categorised Dublin's streets. It allowed the commissioners to see a record of the task before them and made the process of decision making on a city-wide basis both more accurate and clear. It also leads to questions as to why similar studies were not undertaken by the first Paving Board on a regular basis and how, after nine years, the streets of Dublin were still in such bad repair. Owen, in essence, provided the board with the sensory detail available to enable them to make core operational and financial decisions vital to the success of their work.

Important as he may have been to the commissioners' goals, Owen was not infallible. While he was in the process of completing his city survey, a very serious complaint was made about his professional behaviour by a paving contractor, John Duff. Duff had been employed for several years by the Paving Board in the third division, but by April 1783 was under massive financial strain

> having borrowed money [to pay] his men, he was obliged to abscond, being threatened to be thrown into jail; that his furniture was sold by his landlord for rent, & there is more owed him by the corporation than would pay all his debts.[268]

---

267 19 Sept. 1783 (PB/Mins/11, p. 55).
268 19. Apr. 1783 (PB/Mins/10, p. 256).

The cause of this economic hardship stemmed directly from Owen. Despite Duff's repeated requests for Owen to measure the paving he had laid, which was required in order for him to be paid, Owen was simply not doing his daily duties due to the requirements of the city survey. Duff had frequently made arrangements to meet Owen at the site of new paving but, despite often waiting several hours, the surveyor rarely showed up. More troubling, when he did appear he often demanded to be paid by the contractor up to five guineas to complete the work despite being paid 3 per cent per of the overall paver's costs, plus £100 a year by the commissioners to do this work. He was extorting money directly from the paving contractors and being paid twice for the same work. If they refused to pay him, he would simply not measure their work, thus leaving them out of pocket and in financial distress. Owen was essentially running a low-level extortion racket. It may have been only due to his city-wide survey pushing him beyond his capabilities during early 1783 that Owen's misappropriation had been exposed, but there is no telling how long he had been undertaking such dubious practices. Given the questions raised about the murkier elements of the first Paving Board, it is possible that such behaviour may have been going on for quite some time. The second Paving Board, however, was quick to act. Commissioners Richard Annesley and Lord John Luttrell-Olmius Carhampton (1739–1829) proposed a motion to the board that

> the surveyor of this corporation shall not demand or accept of any sum or sums of money for measuring work done in the respective division on pain of dismission for his office ... [and that] their officer shall not take any gratuity whatsoever for measuring works to be performed in the future.[269]

Owen had been caught. The board's not-so-friendly reminder about being dismissed from his post if he was found taking money again was officially entered into the board's minute books in June of that year.[270] However, perhaps in light of the quality of the work he had been doing to date, the commissioners allowed him to enter a memorial every November and 'grant him such allowance as they may think adequate to the extraordinary trouble he may have had in measuring the works made.'[271]

---

269 25 Apr. 1783 (PB/Mins/10, p. 264).
270 27 June 1783 (PB/Mins/11, p. 6).
271 25 Apr. 1783 (PB/Mins/10, p. 264). Owen submitted a request for £18 13s. 6d. in November 1783 as an additional payment owed to him for that year. This was eventually paid, despite the Paving Board's dire financial situation in January 1784.

Familiar problems

Corruption among its employees and inheriting a deeply troubled organisation were not the only difficulties encountered by the second Paving Board. Civil disobediences towards its inspectors and collectors, as encountered by its predecessors, were still disturbingly frequent occurrences. Around the same time as Owen was being dragged over the coals, a collector in the fourth division, in the process of confiscating chairs from a property on Essex Quay, was 'greatly insulted' and had the chairs violently retrieved by their owner. To make matters worse, the constable who had been sent to assist in the seizure gave absolutely no support and the collector was forced to retreat.[272] A far more serious incident occurred the same week in the third division where an inspector of nuisances reported that 'he went to pull down Mr Fitzpatrick's windows, [who] pointed a pistol at him, swearing he would shoot [the inspector] & behaved in a violent & outrageous manner'.[273] The prospect of death for simply removing a street nuisance seems somewhat extreme. However, it was not just the Paving Board's inspectors that were facing down the barrel of a gun as the economic legacy of the first Paving Board came back to haunt them with terminal results. By December 1783 the fiscal reports from each division, coupled with Owen's city survey, presented the commissioners with sombre reading. Unless the Irish parliament was able to provide them with monetary assistance, work in the first, second (Fig. 3.2), third and sixth divisions would not be sustainable. The board had already calculated that no work could take place in the first division for up to fifteen months and in the sixth for up to two years, and that they did not have a sufficient cash flow to support even emergency work in the second and third divisions. The situation was better in the fourth and fifth divisions, but only barely. The Paving Board was facing a financial meltdown:

> it appears to this board, that the present ruinous state of the funds, has originated in the former corporation, which having power to borrow money, carried on their works with such rapidity, as forced them to accumulate a depth, that has involved this corporation in its present distress, for when they entered into office, they found a debt of £33,181.10.6 that bears interest, besides a current debt which did not bear interest of £2,902.13.7.[274]

---

272 6 June 1783 (PB/Mins/10, p. 310).
273 6 June 1783 (PB/Mins/10, p. 309).
274 12 Dec. 1783 (PB/Mins/11, p. 147).

strongly argued that a priority should be afforded to 'streets, quays, and places, several aldermen, common-council men, and committee-men resided, and thereby made convenient ways and passages to their own abodes'.[279] Such misallocation of resources may not have had too large an impact on the Paving Board if their finances had been in better condition; this was not the case, however, and indicates significant organisational mismanagement from the inception of the board.

Thomas Owen was interviewed at length by Blaquiere and went into great detail about the results of his 1783 city survey for the second Paving Board.[280] This survey formed a central argument of the report, as it demonstrated that the financial resources available to the Paving Board were unable to cope with the demands of the work and, coupled with the crippling debt created by the first Paving Board's rampant borrowing, that the organisation simply could not continue to function. It had been stretched beyond the point of recovery. Unsurprisingly, the report's conclusions were damning and its author determined that the streets of Dublin had been 'scandalously neglected' by the Paving Board.[281]

Around the same time that Blaquiere was finishing his investigation, an anonymous article appeared in the *Dublin Evening Post* criticising the work of the Paving Board and airing wider public dissatisfaction with how the project had been handled to date:

> As the beauty and general convenience of this city have of late become objects of national concern ... let us for a moment compare London with Dublin, where I believe the individual is not taxed so highly, and the streets paved in a much superior manner, and we cannot avoid thinking that mismanagement lies somewhere.[282]

Blaquiere's response to his investigation was to propose a radically different set-up for the maintenance of Dublin's streets. Authority would be removed from Dublin Corporation and placed entirely in the hands of six unelected directors who would manage a reformed group of commissioners, divisional and parochial committees. Fines and prison sentences would be issued by the board of directors and commissioners outside of the control of Dublin Corporation, giving this small group immense power over the city's residents. Governance of Dublin's streets was in essence being removed from those elected by the city's citizens to do such

---

279   Evidence of Robert Thorp; ibid., p. 234.
280   Evidence of Thomas Owen; ibid., p. 233.
281   Ibid., p. 236.
282   *Dublin Evening Post*, 8 Apr. 1784.

a task and being privatised. Commissioners could no longer be members of the Irish Parliament and were to meet three times a week, being paid twenty shillings per meeting (working out at £150 per annum). Property taxes would still be used to fund the organisation, but this would now be supplemented by the transfer of duties of 'gentlemen's carriages' from the corporation to the new Paving Board. Blaquiere added that 'The public will therefore judge, [whether] it be wiser to give those allowances, in order to secure this responsibility, or to give no salary and allow such enormous sums of money to be expended in the manner they have been heretofore'.[283]

One issue that the public was already judging before Blaquiere's proposal was the poor economic situation in the country. Much of the economic hardship related to the removal of 'protecting duties' on Irish linen manufacturers. This restricted the sale of Irish linen goods to Europe, an economic mainstay, thus reducing their market considerably and causing substantial turmoil in the industry.[284] Such actions impacted extensively on Ulster where up to one in five adults was involved in linen weaving.[285] The situation grew so bad that Ulster politician William Conyngham (1733–96) resorted to importing large quantities of cornmeal and distributing it to his tenants in Donegal at a greatly reduced price to help relieve their suffering.[286] The newspaper the *Volunteers Journal*, published by Mathew Carey and a mouthpiece for radical liberal elements in Irish politics, commented on the growing hardships at the time as 'We are in extreme poverty in every part of this kingdom ... and having no capital, we can give no credit; not being able to give credit, we cannot export to foreign markets'.[287] The *Dublin Evening Post* added to these feelings by blaming the removal of the duties on the undue influence of the English linen industry and warned of the possibility that anger was so great that revolt was not uncertain:

> Q. From whom did you force the nominal restoration of your rights?
>
> A. The English.
>
> Q. Who bribed your Senate to dispense with the actual enjoyment of them?
>
> A. The English.

---

283 *Freeman's Journal*, 6 Apr. 1784.
284 Anon., *A letter to the linen-manufacturers of Ireland* (Dublin, 1784), p. 7.
285 McBride, *Eighteenth-century Ireland*, p. 109.
286 *Dublin Evening Post*, 8 Apr. 1784.
287 *Volunteers Journal*, 2 Apr. 1784.

Q. Whose gold prevented your Protecting Duties?

A. The English.

Q. Who should cut off the continuance of these evils?

A. Two million of Irishmen in arms.[288]

At the time there were two growing and diametrically opposed camps within parliament: those who supported greater Irish political freedom in the country's affairs and those that wished to bring the Dublin and Westminster governments closer, perhaps even into union. Events in the North American colonies had proven that a nation could overhaul how it was governed, both politically and through force of arms, and had been noted by members of the Irish Patriot Party. The Irish Volunteers, a movement of local militias established during the American Revolutionary War (1775–83) to supplement the British garrison in Ireland, now found itself able to apply significant pressure for increased legislative powers being granted to the Dublin parliament. In November 1779 the Volunteers displayed their strength by holding a mass armed assembly on College Green, immortalised in a painting by Francis Wheatley (1747–1801), demanding greater free trade between Britain and Ireland to help alleviate economic problems. Their pressure helped gain effective legislative independence for Ireland from Britain under the Constitution of 1782 that was spearheaded by Henry Grattan. Much of the political provocation during this era came from the *Volunteers Journal*, which placed blame for the financial turmoil felt in the country on the government, going so far as to advertise a fictitious book called *The whole art and mystery of tarring and feathering a traitor*. This book was dedicated by 'fifty thousand starving manufacturers' to politician and future Paving Board director Henry Luttrell (1743–1821), who the journal blamed for much of the country's financial woes. The political schism was becoming so great that one period newspaper felt the need to remind its readers that others in Europe were watching developments in Ireland and that 'a nation divided in itself must become prey to foreigners'.[289]

288 *Dublin Evening Post*, 8 Apr. 1784.
289 *Freeman's Journal*, 6 Apr. 1784.

4.2   *James Napper Tandy (1740–1803), United Irishman* by James Heath (1815). Stipple (35.4 x 27.5cm). James Napper Tandy was a political agitator and former member of the Dublin Paving Board (NGI 10940; photograph courtesy of the National Gallery of Ireland ©).

Such a tumultuous economic and political state of affairs was an ideal opportunity for middle class liberal radicals such as MP John Binns (*c.*1730–1804) and future United Irishman James Napper Tandy (*c.*1737–1803; Fig. 4.2) to forward their cause for parliamentary reform.[290] Both men had previous experience of the Paving Board as they each served as commissioners during the 1770s and, at the time of Blaquiere's proposal, had vehemently supported the boycotting of foreign goods until the protecting duties were restored.[291] All that was required to ignite the situation was a political and social spark; this came in the form of the Paving Board.

290   James McGuire and James Quinn (eds.), *The dictionary of Irish biography*, 9 vols. (Cambridge, 2009), vol. 9, p. 266.
291   Ibid., 1, p. 546.

College Green paving riot

On Monday 5 April 1784 during the height of the controversy surrounding protecting duties, the Recorder to Dublin Corporation, Alderman Warren, accompanied by the high sheriffs and 'a number of respectable citizens'[292] made the ten-minute walk from the Tholsel, opposite Christchurch Cathedral, to Parliament House on College Green. It was Warren's intention to serve a petition to the government protesting in the strongest possible terms the corporation's dissatisfaction with Blaquiere's paving bill. The corporation felt the bill was an attempt 'to overthrow the chartered privileges of the citizens of Dublin' and was 'against the immediate interests, rights and municipal laws that govern such an extensive community'.[293]

On their way to College Green, the small contingent was joined by a large number of protesting manufacturers, referred to in a period satirical report on the event as 'many idle persons',[294] who had gathered to demonstrate against the state of the linen trade and who had found common cause with the corporation.[295] Upon arriving at their destination, the mob began to verbally abuse, harass and 'justly reproach' the members of parliament entering the building.[296] Among those jostled was Sir Boyle Roche (1736–1807). Roche was a member of parliament opposed to the ideals of Tandy and Binns who had a distinguished military career in North America during the Seven Years War (1756–63) and was so infamous for his mixed metaphors and malapropisms that he earned the moniker 'Lord Boyle Balderdash'.[297] He later complained that when

> he was coming to the House on Monday last, he was stopped by a mob, and enclosed as it were in a vortex, from which he could not get out: they asked who he was, and he told them – they desired to know where he was going? He answered to the Parliament House – they then wanted to swear him against Sir John Blaquiere's bill ... he answered, if he wanted to serve them before, he would act contrary now from their behaviour – he asked them who they were? They said the aggregate. What!

---

292   *Freeman's Journal*, 6 Apr. 1784.
293   Ibid.
294   *Volunteers Journal*, 14 Apr. 1784.
295   Ibid., 7 Apr. 1784.
296   Ibid.
297   Among the anecdotes attributed to Roche are 'Ireland and England are like two sisters; I would have them embrace like one brother', 'Half the lies our opponents tell about us are untrue' and 'All along the untrodden paths of the future, I can see the footprints of an unseen hand.'

Gentlemen, shall the aggregate insult us? – Shall Napper Tandy be able to run into the recesses and environs of their city to bring the aggregate to surround us?[298]

4.3   *The Irish House of Commons, the declaration of Irish Rights by Henry Grattan* by Nicholas Kenny (1782). The Irish House of Commons was the scene of much debate and protest about the Paving Board's future (courtesy of the National Library of Ireland © NLI).

In the midst of this protest, several members of the crowd forced their way into the parliament building and, after making their way to the public gallery overlooking the house of commons, proceeded to 'harangue the members', stating that the 'a member had better meet the devil than an angry weaver'.[299] They demanded that those gathered should be willing

> to share those bribes they had received from England, among the distressed manufacturers ... the chaste ear of the majority [of parliament] was naturally shocked at this *indelicate* insinuation. With the jealous sensibility to groundless reproach, which *conscious innocence* has been ever know to betray, the house instantly took fire at even a suspicion of its virtue.[300]

---

298   *Dublin Journal*, 6 Apr. 1784.
299   *Volunteers Journal*, 7 Apr. 1784.
300   Ibid.

Two of the protestors were arrested in the gallery, while outside on College Green events grew even more heated.[301] With the parliaments' own small force outnumbered and overwhelmed, a body of troops had to be summoned to suppress the protest and disperse the crowd, described in a predisposed *Volunteers Journal* report:

> [The protestors] would in all probability have proceeded to lay violent hands on some *very deserving* members, if a body of the military, consisting of horse and foot, had not, in the most orderly and humane manner, put those bloody minded people to the bayonet and by pouring in their heavy cavalry on the broken multitude obtained, notwithstanding the evident disparity of numbers, *a complete and decisive victory over the unarmed and defenceless citizens.*[302]

There are no known records of casualties of this event but with the city placed under temporary military control, the protest's shockwaves reverberated around Dublin for weeks to come.

Despite the disruption that the mob had caused, Alderman Warren proceeded with serving Dublin Corporation's petition to parliament. He protested that the new paving bill was against the chartered rights and privileges of the corporation over the city and was 'a system of unexampled tyranny and oppression'.[303] The new powers granted to 'a set of low persons (for commissioners acting for £150 a year could be no other)' huge legal power and under the act 'the father would be compelled to give evidence against this son, the son against his father'.[304]

The government responded by reminding the Alderman that the corporation should not 'let their petitions be brought in upon the flying clamour of an *infamous* mob'.[305] It insinuated that the riot had been started by members of the corporation involved with the Paving Board hoping to distract attention from their financial mismanagement or trying to intimidate parliament. Dublin lord mayor Thomas Green was also blamed as he 'suffered, without opposition, mobs to parade the streets'[306] and did not intervene; however, the parochial committees of the city

---

301 Ibid., Cornelius Cashel and Richard Barnes. Cashel was subsequently referred to as 'Cashman' in the following edition of the *Volunteers Journal*.
302 Ibid., 14 Apr. 1784.
303 *Freeman's Journal*, 6 Apr. 1784.
304 Ibid.
305 *Volunteers Journal*, 7 Apr. 1784.
306 *Freeman's Journal*, 6 Apr. 1784.

were quick to defend him and his restraint against the protestors.[307] Referring to the collapse of the previous paving boards, John Foster MP (1740–1828) warned Alderman Warren that

> if the city of Dublin misapplied, or did not exert their chartered rights, in preserving the peace of the city, they no longer deserved them, but they ought to be vested in *other hands*, who knew better how to apply them.[308]

Blaquiere adamantly defended his bill, saying that if the corporation continued to run the Paving Board, the citizens of Dublin would be spending most of their paving taxes on repaying the loans taken out by that body and that the fines to be issued by the third Paving Board, some up to forty shillings, were necessary as 'experience had shown that less would not enforce obedience.' He concluded by dismissing the corporation's and protestors' complaints of losing power:

> Our liberty is in danger, because the officer of the board is empowered to levy one shilling; and our rights are destroyed, because our dirt is removed. These were crying grievances indeed, and he hoped the spirit of the aggregate body would not submit to them.[309]

One MP raised suspicions that Blaquiere or other members of parliament may become commissioners and gradually increase the salary for those positions, but Blaquiere was quick to note that there was a clause in the bill to prevent this from happening. Unfortunately, he strategically failed to remind his colleagues that they could become directors of the new Paving Board instead.[310] With discussions in parliament continuing, the military was kept on the streets throughout the night. The city had in effect been placed under temporary martial law, as the *Volunteers Journal* mocked 'To preserve the FREEDOM of debate, and give validity to their proceedings'.[311] With the government still angry about the earlier invasion by protestors, and further inflamed by statements as the one above, the press were also seen as prime culprits by the House of Commons for helping to encourage the rioters with their anti-parliament rhetoric. Newspaper cartoons published at the time showing a man named 'Jacky Finance' (aka John Foster MP) on a gallows in front of parliament house under the title 'Thus perish all traitors to this

---

307 *Volunteers Journal*, 16 Apr. 1784.
308 Ibid., 7 Apr. 1784.
309 *Freeman's Journal*, 6 Apr. 1784.
310 *Dublin Journal*, 6 Apr. 1784.
311 *Volunteers Journal*, 14 Apr. 1784.

country' did little to calm matters and the powers-that-be reacted swiftly.[312] Foster produced in front of the commons 'a paper entitled the *Volunteers Journal*, of this date containing certain libellous paragraphs' and sent a small detachment of men to arrest its publisher Mathew Carey for his seditious comments.[313] Tipped off about his pending imprisonment, Carey was found hiding on the third story of his premises on Abbey Street, but in the same style as his dramatic writing, threw himself out of a nearby window and made his escape down a nearby laneway.[314] The following week an article appeared in the *Volunteers Journal* mocking Foster's attempt to detain him 'The serjeant at arms, and two doorkeepers, *the whole constitutional force of that august body* [parliament], were dispatched to apprehend certain obnoxious printers'.[315] The *Dublin Evening Post* was also quick to attack Foster and his attempt to curtail the freedom of the press:

> The liberty of the press is the prerogative of the people, and like that of the crown, to be exerted for the good of the people, where the laws are silent. A kingdom cannot be in a greater state of slavery, than where it is suppressed.[316]

With a reward on his head Carey eventually handed himself in and was placed under the detention of parliament. A legal loophole allowed the lord mayor to set him free but, finding himself under near-constant observation and fearing further arrest, he emigrated to the United States in September 1784.[317] In the end the control of the nation's newspapers was limited to now including the real name of the publisher on the cover of each issue.

The riot that erupted on College Green in April 1784 was not specifically about the paving bill. The bill represented an opportunity for the press, unemployed manufacturers and Dublin Corporation to vent anger towards the Irish parliament for their own specific hardships. They felt sidelined, ignored and exploited by a wealthy elite that was seen to be slowly eroding their rights. Blaquiere's paving bill was simply a convenience. From parliament's perspective, the direct threats in the *Volunteers Journal*, coupled with an angry and vocal mob, represented a distinct risk to the social order. With memories of the American Revolution still fresh in their

---

312   Ibid., 7 Apr. 1784.
313   Ibid.
314   *Dublin Evening Press*, 8 Apr. 1784.
315   Ibid., 14 Apr. 1784.
316   Ibid., 8 Apr. 1784.
317   James Green, *Mathew Carey* (Philadelphia, 1985), p. 4.

minds, they had observed that civil disobedience and political upheaval by radicals could lead to violent revolt against the system and were quick to stamp out any resistance to their authority.

Despite its difficult birth, Blaquiere's bill passed and Dublin Corporation found its influence over its own streets, and the newly formed Paving Board, greatly diminished. Along with the dramatic demise of local authority control, the chaotic events of 1784 also spelled the beginning of the end of Thomas Owen's career as a surveyor.

1784–7: the third Paving Board

The new 'corporation for paving, cleansing & lighting the streets of Dublin' first met in mid-September 1784 at their offices at 3 South Frederick Street.[318] Most of the summer had been lost to reorganising the Paving Board and the amount of time left for paving work that year was limited. The body was set up under a two tier system of managerial control and was governed by five directors – Lord Ranelagh, James Agar, Sir John Blaquiere, John Leigh, Thomas St George Esq. and General Henry Luttrell. This group met jointly with a group of commissioners – James Ormsby, William Lightburn, William Alexander, John Hall and Hugh Henry Mitchell – and together they issued instructions to divisional and parochial committees throughout the city. The divisional makeup of Dublin had not changed since the time of the second Paving Board and the third Paving Board simply inherited its predecessor's existing operational structure.

The new body was a far more streamlined organisation than its predecessors.[319] Meetings were smaller, usually attended by the majority of the commissioners and occasionally by one or two directors when need arose, which represented a significant change from the crowded sessions of the first Paving Board. By December 1784 the new board found that the amount of work required made it necessary to have daily meetings (rather than the initially prescribed three per week) that could be attended by members of the public.[320] Resident committees were also encouraged to attend meetings relevant to their areas so the board could 'be understood in the most express terms' and confusion thus avoided.[321] The inhabitants of Parliament and Essex Streets were once chastised by the commissioners for failing to attend a meeting about the proposed repaving of their streets, as the board wanted to inform them that once their new paving work had been completed, they would not

---

318   14 Sept. 1784 (PB/Mins/13, p. 2).
319   See appendix for members of the Dublin Paving Boards (1774–87).
320   1 Dec. 1784 (PB/Mins/13, p. 170).
321   15 Mar. 1785 (PB/Mins/14, p. 173).

suffer the road to be opened again, except in the case of great emergency, such as fire.[322] The new board was ready to stamp its authority on the city in a significantly more assertive manner than its predecessors.

One of the duties to fall under the Paving Board's new mandate was the erection and maintenance of a network of public fountains throughout the city. This was a vital public service as, despite the work of the PWC to improve water supply, a large portion of the populace was dependent on public wells and fountains for their drinking and domestic water purposes.[323] This new responsibility was one of the third Paving Board's success stories and by 1786 the board had been empowered to create 'such number of fountains, or conduits, for the supply of water, as they should think necessary' in addition to the original twenty allowed by parliament.[324] Poorly constructed fountains and water leakage could also cause significant problems, as was noted by one early nineteenth-century guide to the city:

> Many great improvements have been made by [the Paving Board]; there were formerly in almost every street one or two fountains, which, though a great ornament, were a great nuisance and the cause of many sad accidents, as they were always crowded by the idle, and the pavement around was so wet and slippery, that horses, particularly in harness, have frequently fallen in attempting to pass, and in winter these places became a perfect sheet of ice.[325]

Citizens caught damaging a fountain or accused of doing so by a credible witness could be fined up to five pounds or imprisoned if they were unable to pay.[326]

There is no record of Owen's activities during the Paving Board's summer hiatus and he took no part in the events of April 1784 except from his interview as part of Blaquiere's report to parliament on the activities of the second Paving Board. He may have continued his role of supervising and measuring repaved streets in a reduced capacity during this time, or he could have found himself without employment; however, with the resumption of the Paving Board, he found his skills again in great demand. The new board requested Owen to produce a thematically coloured map of the city that distinguished streets that had been paved, were under repair or with only temporary works on them, in addition to

---

322 Ibid.
323 25 Geo. III, c. 108 [Ire.] (1786).
324 26 Geo. III, c. 61 [Ire.] (1786).
325 Curry, *The picture of Dublin*, p. 98.
326 Ibid., p. 122.

streets where new street lamps, often referred to as 'globes', had been placed.[327] He was asked to perform the same task a year later, indicating that the Paving Board now wished to keep a better cartographic record of the work accomplished during the previous twelve months and to better measure their progress.[328] Owen was also kept busy with the measurement of streets that the commissioners wished to pave, including the Liffey quays[329] and the North Circular Road,[330] indicating that they were following the example of the London Paving Board and showing more financial caution than their predecessors.[331]

Street lighting

A notable change in the minute books of the third Paving Board was its attention to lighting. Street lamps and globes were rarely, if ever, mentioned in the Paving Board's records prior to 1784 as control of street lighting lay primarily with each parish. This vital public service was now placed under the authority of the Paving Board administration that hired contractors to undertake the nightly task of lighting lamps and ensuring that they stay lit during the hours of darkness. Dominant figures in the Dublin lamps business included contractors John Bray and John Boshell who, along with Bray's father-in-law Peter Howard and silent partner William Bell, set to work on lighting the city at a cost of £1 1s. per globe.[332] To ensure the lighting work was well done, the board employed a number of lighting inspectors including Peter Tone, father of United Irishman and leader of the 1798 rebellion Theobald Wolfe Tone, who was in its employment at £50 a year from the late 1780s onwards. Wolfe Tone referred to his father acquiring the position as 'good fortune' after a family legal dispute had nearly left Peter destitute, but noted that his new role only 'secures him a decent, tho' moderate, independence'.[333]

---

327   26 Oct. 1784 (PB/Mins/13, p. 94).
328   15 Jan. 1785 (PB/Mins/14, p. 20).
329   21 Oct. 1785 (PB/Mins/16, p. 177).
330   1 Nov. 1786 (PB/Mins/19, p. 57).
331   13 Sept. 1785 (PB/Mins/15, p. 63).
332   LaTouche, et al., *Report of the commissioners*, p. 10.
333   T.W. Moody, R.B. McDowell and C.J. Woods (eds.), *The writings of Theobald Wolfe Tone, 1763–98*, vol. 2 (Oxford, 2009), p. 282.

4.4   *View from Capel Street looking over Essex Bridge* by James Malton (1797). This image shows a lamplighter working on Essex Bridge, Dublin (courtesy of the National Library of Ireland © NLI).

Like scavengers, the professional life of a lamplighter had a significant rough-and-tumble element to it. Contractors had to walk a tight line between providing a service that the Paving Board would be satisfied with on sometimes dangerous streets, while also trying to keep their overheads to an absolute minimum to increase profits. Authority over public lighting in Dublin since the 1690s had varied from being under complete control of Dublin Corporation,[334] to its privatisation in 1717 by two merchants, William Aldrich and Hugh Cumming,[335] and its eventual reversion to parochial control in 1759 with support from local taxation.[336] By the time the third Paving Board came into being in the 1780s, there were almost ten thousand lamps in the city and lamplighters were a common sight on Dublin's streets each evening. One was even included in the background of one of James Malton's (1761–1801) well-known Dublin street scenes, perched on a ladder

---

334   9 Will. III, c. 17 [Ire.] (1697).
335   4 Geo. I, c. 9 ss 6–11 [Ire.] (1717).
336   33 Geo. II, c. 18 [Ire.] (1759).

attending to lamps on Essex Bridge (Fig. 4.4). Lamplighters like Malton's fuelled and ignited the oil-fed street lights each night, accessing them with ladders, and patrolled their assigned districts to relight any lamp that went dark, as summed up in a contemporary poem:

'Tis then the Lamp-lighter renews his toil,

And trims the cotton, and pours in the oil;

Clean keep the globe, like crystal to the eye,

The short'liv'd light of Phoebus to supply.[337]

To enforce their terms with contractors any lamp found not lit by a Paving Board inspector would result in a fine. In order to avoid these fines, John Bray placed adverts in the Dublin newspapers encouraging residents of the city to visit his office on Fishamble Street and report 'neglect of duty in the lighters' thus hoping to bypass the inspector's attention.[338] This approach came into being following a spot inspection by the Paving Board in December 1786. On one weekend alone, the Paving Board's lighting inspectors noted that up to 3,500 globes were unlit across the city, representing just over a third of all street lights. Such lack of service was an issue the Paving Board would be unable to hide due to its highly public nature. The commissioners issued a notice in the *Dublin Journal* informing the public of the 'shameful manner' in which the lighting contractors had performed recently and that they were to be fined one shilling per lamp found unlit, coming to a combined total of £178 2s.[339] This figure, when put into perspective, represented almost two years wages for some of the Paving Board's better-paid employees such as Owen or secretary Richard Gladwell.

For funding, each building in the city was required to pay a lamp tax based on the value of the property. Every house valued above £20 was required to pay 1s. 6d. per year, valuations between £10 and £20 were 1s., with the rest at 12d. per pound of annual rent.[340] In total, the combined revenue from paving and lighting tax was in the region of £14,000 per year between 1784 and 1787;[341] however, the commissioners still felt it necessary to take out a loan of £2,000 in late 1784.[342] The earl of Meath and the archbishop of Dublin were both granted special dispensation in the liberties of Thomas Court, Donore and St Sepulchre's in the fifth, sixth and

---

337   Anon., *The lamplighter's poem* (London, c.1794).
338   *Dublin Journal*, 21 Dec. 1786.
339   19 Dec. 1786 (PB/Mins/19, p. 157); *Dublin Journal*, 20 Dec. 1786.
340   *Freeman's Journal*, 1 Apr. 1784; 31 Jan. 1785 (PB/Mins/14, p. 67).
341   LaTouche, et al., *Report of the commissioners*, p. 64.
342   22 Dec. 1784 (PB/Mins/13, p. 229).

former seventh divisions under the 1784 paving bill. These areas of the city paid their own local lamp tax and were considered outside the jurisdiction of Paving Board lighting until new changes were implemented in 1805.[343]

Early lamp work undertaken by the Paving Board was well received by the citizens of Dublin, with one commentator stating the number of street robberies had significantly decreased since the new paving act took place.[344] However, not all reviews of the Paving Board's work were as positive. In October 1785, the parochial committee of St Nicholas Within (see Fig. 4.5) after having little success through official channels to the commissioners about lamps not being lit over a two-week period, placed an advert in the *Dublin Journal* complaining that:

> It is a very intolerable grievance that the inhabitants of this parish are obliged to pay such an enormous increase of tax for light ... when there has been no more than two additional lamps erected in this parish since the commencement of the late act ... [and] that the present contractors for lighting, or persons employed under them, have been shamefully negligent in the execution of their business.[345]

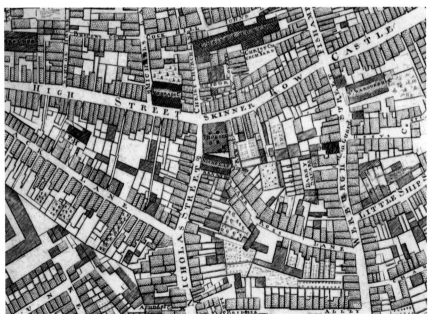

4.5   The parish of St. Nicholas Within (from John Rocque, *An exact survey of the city of Dublin* (1756), courtesy of the Board of Trinity College Dublin).

343   *Dublin Journal*, 14 Sept. 1784.
344   Ibid., 28 Sept. 1784.
345   Ibid., 11 Oct. 1785.

The Paving Board was quick to answer such strong criticism of their work in a public forum. In a response, Paving Board secretary Gladwell wrote that its taxation was entirely fair as it was means tested against property value; the commissioners were also eager to note that they had significantly improved the lighting conditions in the city during their short tenure to date:

> The board will not enter into particulars, but the generous public will judge whether any improvement in the lighting of the city has been made or not. The fact is, that previous to the establishment of this board, there were in the whole city but 2,247 single lights, at this moment the number of single lights burning in this city amount to no less than 10,220. Where the former were well, and these ill maintained, it is not for the board to say.[346]

The board felt that their contractors were taking 'every possible exertion' to fulfil their role, but accepted that there were issues in keeping all lamps in the city lit. The 'enormous increase of tax' was also the subject of a complaint from a resident of Merrion Square. The resident, during his rambling complaint, unfortunately noted that he had been dodging his civic duties for years by not paying, saying 'that he would have complained before but not having paid any tax, he did not consider himself called upon or instilled to complain'.[347] No matter what exertion the contractors took, theirs was not an easy task. Being a lamplighter was a difficult job, as it required patrolling the streets nightly, in all weathers, seeking out unlit sections of the city. It also left them highly venerable to assaults, accidents and injury while exposed on their ladders attending to the lamps, particularly by passing traffic, as mentioned in a poem from the era:

> Sometimes when busied on the ladder's top,
> The slipp'ry ice will make the ladder drop:
> Or, while he's heedless of the dread approach,
> Of cart, or dray, or chariot, or of coach,
> The carless driver against the ladder runs,
> And both the ladder and the man o'erturns:
> Thus by the fall he gets a dreadful knock,
> By which he's kill'd, or else his bones are broke,
> And while your lampman on the ground does lie,
> The guilty driver hastes himself away;
> Leaving the man he maim'd in sad despair,

---

346 Ibid., 15 Oct. 1785; 17 Oct. 1785 (PB/Mins/16, p. 165).
347 25 Aug. 1785 (PB/Mins/16, p. 18).

Unto some christian's hospitable care;
Then to a surgeon kind perhaps he's bore,
With fractur'd bones, or else some bleeding sore;
And while he's there, or what is worse, is dead,
His helpless wife and children crie for bread:
Thus many accidents we do receive,
More than most people really would believe.[348]

From 1784 onwards the minute books of the Paving Board are littered with reports of sabotage, assaults and hit-and-run incidents related to lamplighters on an almost weekly basis (Fig. 4.6).

Much of the violence towards lamplighters came in the form of general vandalism, particularly in breaking the glass globes and lamps late at night. The new Paving Board was keen to assert its authority on the matter with fines and prison sentences being issued on nearly every occasion that a perpetrator was apprehended. Such was the case for William Alcock, who was arrested on Ormond Quay and fined forty shillings by the commissioners for breaking a globe. When he was unable to produce the payment, he was sentenced to the Bridewell prison for three months.[349] He was released after being able to raise the money and his fine was distributed between the watchmen who had apprehended him and the lamplighters to repair the damage that he had done.[350]

4.6   A series of images highlighting the dangers faced by eighteenth-century lamplighters (from Thomas Sabine, *The Lamplighter's poem* (c.1770), © The Trustees of the British Museum).

---

348   Anon., *The lamplighter's poem* (London, c.1760).
349   5 Nov. 1784 (PB/Mins/13, p. 116).
350   19 Nov. 1784 (PB/Mins/13, p. 123).

The city's resident military population was also prone to damaging street lamps. The board's first complaint to the local army commander regarding lamps came shortly after it began work in 1784. It was noted that troops were breaking lamps when marching with their weapons sloped, presumably with fixed bayonets; however, no one was able to determine if the damage had been done maliciously or by accident. Lamps were ordered to be raised in height to reduce such future breakage.[351] Two months later, the army was again found to be responsible for damage, namely by several officers who early one morning were witnessed smashing around a dozen lamps on Arran Quay. They were pursued by the local watchmen and lamplighters but were able to escape into their barracks. This situation left Grenadier John Flynn of the Twenty-Sixth Regiment in a very difficult situation. He happened to be sentry that night at the barracks and was requested by the Paving Board to supply the identities of the officers responsible for the damage. If he identified them then he ran the risk of being victimised by his superior officers, but if he failed to comply the commissioners threatened to inform the commander-in-chief of his non-cooperation.[352] No record is made of the result of Flynn's difficult decision.

Lamplighters were also occasionally not the victims but rather the perpetrators of criminal acts. In 1785, one was fined £10 for selling his lamp oil,[353] another was pushed off his ladder and beaten by a colleague who was subsequently imprisoned,[354] and even the main contractor, John Bray, was accused of intimidating his lamplighters by enforcing his own business acumen on his men 'to see that one man's work does not burn better than another.'[355] But regardless of such infringements the lighters were usually at the receiving end of illegal incidents.

Despite being one of the premium commercial thoroughfares in the city during this era, Capel Street was the scene of many of the more serious assaults on lamplighters (see Fig. 4.7). In September 1785, a lamplighter was beaten up by a group of men and, even though he begged for help, the local residents and passers-by failed to come to his assistance.[356] An assault on one of the Paving Board's employees was an assault on the institution itself and the new board was more than willing to make an example of the Capel Street residents as an example to others. In response to the lack of help offered to their lamplighter, the Paving Board ordered that no lamps were to be lit on the street the following night as a form of punishment to the residents. In the future they would either assist lamplighters in distress or they

---

351   19 Oct. 1784 (PB/Mins/13, p. 76).
352   3 Dec. 1784 (PB/Mins/13, p. 176).
353   28 Oct. 1785 (PB/Mins/16, p. 198).
354   3 Sept. 1785 (PB/Mins/16, p. 40).
355   Evidence of Steward Fitzpatrick; 27 Sept. 1785 (PB/Mins/16, p. 107).
356   7 Sept. 1785 (PB/Mins/16, p. 50).

would have such services removed. Other areas of the city were quick to take note of Capel Street's punishment with even the relatively trouble-free parishes of St Nicholas Within and St Michan's both writing to the board saying they would accompany their local lamplighters to ensure their safety.[357]

4.7   Capel Street often proved a hazardous area for Paving Board employees (from John Rocque, *An exact survey of the city of Dublin* (1756), courtesy of the Board of Trinity College Dublin).

357   13 Sept. 1785 (PB/Mins/16, p. 59).

The inhabitants of the offending street apparently took their punishment to heart. A week later, lamplighter Peter Borsey was set upon in the early evening by a William Hackett on Capel Street. Hackett followed Borsey from lamp to lamp, insulting him and trying to raise a mob against the lighter. James Gamble, the local inspector of nuisances, was on nearby Little Strand Street when

> he heard the lamplighter calling for help; & when he went to see what was the matter, he saw Jane Bradshaw holding the boy's ladder ... & obstructing him when acting under the Board in the prosecution of his duty; & having apprehended her, he was molested by Charles Shiel in Castle Street, who said he would cook him, & endowed to foment riot by raising mobs in the street, & that he also apprehended the said Charles Shiel, & that he was assisted in his duty by the inhabitants of Capel Street, without whose help he would have been violently opposed.[358]

Hackett, Shiel and Bradshaw were sent to the Bridewell for being unable to pay a fine of £5 each. Despite being saved during this incident, lamplighter Borsey's career was unfortunately cut short the following year in a similar incident when a group of men pushed him from his ladder, again on Capel Street. He was severely injured.[359]

Why such violence was directed against lamplighters is unknown. They were members of the community well known to the residents of the streets in which they worked, so assaults may have stemmed from personal disagreements. Excessive alcohol consumption from passers-by may also have played a factor (as the lamplighters worked exclusively at night) or the events may simply have been the result of general hooliganism or resentment against lighting taxes. Unfortunately the commissioners failed to elaborate on the causes of these events, simply dealing with their damaging consequences. The Paving Board acknowledged that the work its employees undertook, particularly at night, left them vulnerable to assaults, and took active steps towards helping protect them by officially requesting that the lord mayor supply their inspectors of nuisances with two or three peace officers 'finding their [employees] are sometimes obliged to go into parts of the town, where difficulty sometimes is in enforcing the laws'.[360] This appeal came about not only due to the ongoing assaults on the lamplighters but also incidents including one involving a tax collector in the fifth division who had been set upon by a

---

358   14 Sept. 1785 (PB/Mins/16, p. 68).
359   4 Nov. 1785 (PB/Mins/16, p. 211).
360   12 Apr. 1785 (PB/Mins/14, p. 252).

drunken crowd that had threatened to tar and feather him or the macabre act of a man who charged members of the public to see the corpse of a vagrant he had found in his stables. The commissioners technically considered the corpse to be an obstruction as it had been placed on the footpath, drawing a considerable crowd.[361]

Constabulary assistance, as has already been noted, varied from parish to parish, thus the security of Paving Board employees was far from certain. By the mid-1780s, the Paving Board had become so frustrated by this situation that it had received supporting legislation making it a finable offence for a constable or watchman to ignore or refuse to help Paving Board employees in distress. For serious breaches of this ruling, constables could be sent 'to the house of correction, there to be kept to hard labour for any time not exceeding seven days'.[362] More substantial protection came into being in 1786 with the foundation of the Dublin Metropolitan Police (DMP).[363] This force, readily supported by Paving Board directors Sir John Blaquiere and Lord Ranelagh,[364] replaced the traditional city watchmen who had been responsible for security on Dublin's streets since the fourteenth century. Watchmen operated within the city's patchwork of parochial boundaries, whereas the new DMP was divided into four large police divisions that covered the entire city, two north and two south of the Liffey, with their headquarters at 8 South William Street.[365] Their jurisdiction was bounded by the north and south circular roads and, armed with their muskets and bayonets, the DMP represented a significant step towards the modernisation of Dublin's law enforcement.[366]

The DMP had a vested interest in the activities of the Paving Board's lamplighters. Well-lit streets helped reduce crime as it removed hiding places from perpetrators while creating greater opportunities to identify criminals. This was noted in one of the many poems related to the life of lamplighters from the era:

> What mischief else, what terror would you meet,
> In each unguarded alley, lane, or street,
> What murders, robb'ries, rapes would else be made,
> Were but your Lampmen to forsake their trade.[367]

---

361   14 Oct. 1784 (PB/Mins/16, p. 159); 20 Mar. 1787 (PB/Mins/19, p. 278).
362   25 Geo. III, c. 108 [Ire.] (1786).
363   26 Geo. III, c. 24 [Ire.] (1786).
364   28 Jan. 1785 (PB/Mins/14, p. 58).
365   Jim Herlihy, *The Dublin metropolitan police* (Dublin, 2001), p. 5.
366   Ibid., p. 6.
367   Anon., *The lamplighter's poem* (London, c.1760).

Poorly maintained lighting could result in alarm from neighbourhoods over a potential upsurge in crime. The residents of Dominick Street were quite vocal on this issue, informing the Paving Board that 'they are extremely apprehensive of being greatly exposed to robbers, on [account] of their being insufficient lights, especially at the corners of lanes'.[368] In October 1786, one of the three city police commissioners followed up on this problem, informing the Paving Board that the chief constable of the Barrack Division had noted that lamps were not lit along Church Street. The commissioners passed on their thanks to the police for alerting them to this issue and informed their contractors that

> the board will fine very heavily if [contractors] do not strictly attend to the business of the & prevent future complaints as the inhabitants say they will themselves come forward hereafter & prove their complaints.[369]

Despite providing a useful check on the work of their lamplighters and protection for their officers on the street, the Paving Board occasionally found it necessary to complain about the DMP. In one incident lamplighter Daniel Parkinson was attending to his duties very early on a Sunday morning on Dawson Street when he was pushed from his ladder by two assailants – William and John Whealy. Running from his attackers, he sought shelter at the local watch house being guarded by DMP constable Christopher Chapman. Chapman apprehended the Whealys but failed to search or secure his prisoners properly. One of the Whealys, seeing an opportunity to continue their assault on Parkinson: 'without any provocation he started up & with the loaded end of his whip he struck [Parkinson] on the head and wounded him desperately'.[370] The Paving Board was swift in filing a complaint with the DMP over the incident and was surprised that a prisoner who had assaulted one of their employees could behave with such 'delinquency' while in custody.[371] The Whealys were fined the unusually large sum of £15 by the Paving Board. Even with police protection it seems that the life of a lamplighter was still fraught with danger.

Events such as Parkinson's beating or the litany of incidents on Capel Street highlight not only the dangers Paving Board staff and contactors had to endure in order to keep the city lit at night, but also the power the commissioners had over the city's populous. If the Paving Board was to execute its duties it, and its officers, needed to be respected. Such respect could only be gained through the possibility

---

368   3 Oct. 1785 (PB/Mins/16, p. 124).
369   17 Oct. 1786 (PB/Mins/19, p. 31).
370   9 Jan. 1787 (PB/Mins/19, p. 181).
371   11 Jan. 1787 (PB/Mins/19, p. 185).

of punishment for non-compliance. The power to fine and imprison individuals or to remove services from whole sections of the city without an independent appeals process gave the commissioners significant authority over the city and brought weight to the arguments posed by Dublin Corporation against the setting up of the third Paving Board during the 1784 parliamentary debate. The commissioners were, in the process of supplying vital services to the city, in effect a law unto themselves.

Thomas Owen's downfall (1784–7)

With Dublin's lamps diverting much of the third Paving Board's attention, Thomas Owen found himself very busy with material inspection during 1784–6. As surveyor, Owen's construction and architectural background was employed to review the quality of material used to pave Dublin' streets and his opinion carried much weight in this matter. Trying to avoid the use of recycled material in street repair as much as possible, the Paving Board looked to stone merchants to provide their paving stone. One of the Paving Board's main suppliers was a Mr John Gowan who sourced materials from both Guernsey and Wicklow.[372]

In December 1784 Owen and Commissioner John Hall made a field trip to Wicklow to inspect Gowan's quarries and to see if they could identify issues that had led to a series of delays in supplying material. Their first visit was to the townland of Ballinacarrick, near Arklow. They found seventeen of Gowan's men at work who had laid out nearly five hundred square yards of material 'finished in a superior quality' to be carried around half a kilometre to the coast for transport.[373] The use of sea transport was vital to such quarrying operations and Dublin's status as a port city greatly aided the process of paving its streets. Materials can only be mined where they are located, thus limiting the source of origin for the Paving Board's stone. Ideally a source closer to Dublin would have reduced material costs, but the Arklow quarries were the nearest site for the quality of stone sought. A further constriction meant that due to the country's poor road system and lack of land transportation to move such a large quantity of material, the quarries supplying the commissioners needed to be close to the sea. Sea transport was a significantly cheaper and more efficient method of moving large quantities of such heavy material and radically reduced the cost per ton moved.

372 1 Sept. 1785 (PB/Mins/16, p. 34) [Guernsey]; 6 Dec. 1784 (DCA/PB/Mins/13, p. 176) [Wicklow].
373 Ibid.

Owen and Hall observed the quarry workers 'going on with great industry and attention' and felt that any delay in supplying stone from this site had more to do with the quality of the material rather than with the work force, which included four skilled stone masons from Glasgow. The site at Ballinacarrick was subleased by Gowan from a tenant and the Paving Board was keen to reach a deal with the landlord to secure mining rights in perpetuity for the lease, thus securing a long-term source for materials.[374]

The pair then continued to another site nearby in Ballinaclay which they found to be 'of excellent, if not superior quality to the other, and of which these are more promising appearances should the other fail as they enter deep into the rock'.[375] It is important to remember that the extent of the Paving Board was much greater than what was visible on the streets of Dublin. Without the work of Gowan's men toiling away on hillsides in Wicklow, or the supply-chain process of moving such large quantities of stone from quarries to ships and from Dublin Port to storage yards, the paving and repair of the city's streets would have been significantly impacted. A particularly harsh winter in 1786 was responsible for flooding many of the Paving Board's quarries and practically halted all but emergency repair work in the city once the stored supplies had run out.[376] During this period, Owen was asked to make an urgent inspection of works throughout the city and to identify which ones were of absolute necessity to help conserve their limited materials.[377] The same cold snap also found the Paving Board recommending to the public that their coal-stoppers,[378] still visible on many of Dublin's Georgian-era streets (Fig. 4.8), should have a rough face 'to prevent danger of people slipping in wet & frosty weather'.[379]

---

374 Ibid.
375 Ibid.
376 11 Dec. 1786 (PB/Mins/19, p. 145).
377 12 Dec. 1786 (PB/Mins/19, p. 146).
378 Small chutes leading from street level to the basement of each house to allow coal deliveries.
379 30 Dec. 1786 (PB/Mins/19, p. 169).

experience like others who had held the role in the past, Brownrigg was a land surveyor with extensive knowledge of engineering works. His professional lineage was about as good as possible for an Irish survey practitioner of that era. He was a former pupil and business partner of the highly successful estate surveyor Bernard Scalé (1738–1826), who in turn had been assistant to John Rocque, creator of the high watermark of eighteenth-century Irish cartography *An exact survey of Dublin* (Dublin, 1756). At the time of his employment with the Paving Board, Brownrigg was partnered with Thomas Sherrard, surveyor and secretary to the Dublin WSC and based out of its surveying and land valuation business in Capel Street.[399] Perhaps Brownrigg's greatest contribution to the work of the Paving Board was the creation of a street plan of Dublin in 1799 by division, of which only one copy is known to have survived (Fig. 5.1). Brownrigg's map represents the last great eighteenth-century survey of Dublin, joining the likes of John Rocque (1756) and Charles Brooking (1728), and provides a closer view of the city's layout than was often unavailable from generic period street plans. His surviving map, representing the fifth division, provides distinct views of both the dense urban core and tree-lined country lanes only two kilometres apart. Notable buildings such as churches, meeting houses and the city workhouse were distinguished from their surrounds with a solid infill as well as being individually named, while ordinary buildings were merged into city blocks, focusing the reader's attention on the street layout. Brownrigg's inclusion of magnetic variation[400] in his north arrow may indicate that he used a circumferentor to conduct his work, while the map appears to have been a unique manuscript as all features are hand-drawn and coloured.

---

399   Wilson, Peter, *Wilsons' Dublin directory* (Dublin, 1783–1800).
400   The difference between true north and magnetic north. This variation changes yearly due to the movement of the magnetic poles and would have affected a circumferentor's measurements as its reference point, i.e. magnetic north, would migrate. By denoting the variation at the time of measurement, Brownrigg ensured that his survey could be easily compared to others from a time when the magnetic variation was different.

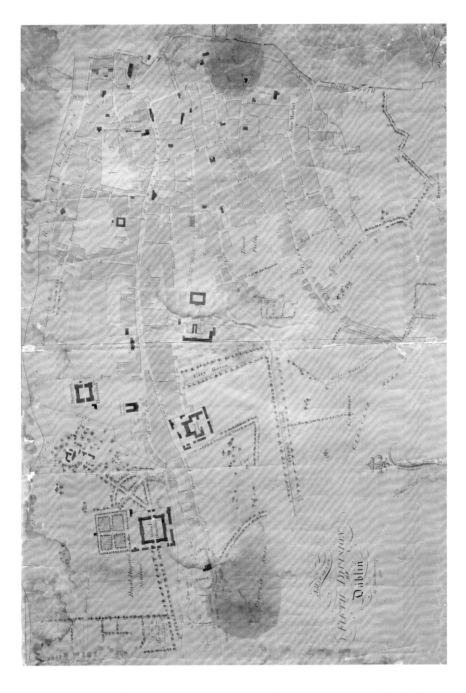

5.1　*Map of the fifth division* by John Brownrigg (1799). Brownrigg's map of the fifth division is a good example of his surveying talent and a rare case of cartographic output from the Paving Board (courtesy of Dublin City Council ©).

It is interesting to note the difference between the work of Owen and Brownrigg at this juncture. Both were requested by the commissioners to produce city surveys; however, this request helps define the professional differences and strengths between Owen's architectural and building background and Brownrigg's surveying one. Owen's 1782 survey was entirely numerical with lists of widths, lengths and areas placed against street names, very much resembling a ledger, while Brownrigg's was cartographically based. Both are correct. Both represent the city and are equally informative; it is simply their delivery method that differs. The human brain is, however, more inclined to interpret Brownrigg's street layout, rather than a list of figures, as a representation of the city. Owen was capable of making high-quality visual plans, as seen by his work for the duke of Leinster (see Figs 1.4 and 1.5), but it is unknown if he would have been accomplished enough to create a map as vast as Brownrigg's. The difference between the two projects probably lay in the commissioners' requirements. Owen's 1782 survey was a stocktaking exercise to calculate a final figure in square feet and inches, thus allowing a vital financial number to be placed on what it would take to pave Dublin's streets. Brownrigg's 1799 survey allowed planning and easier visual interpretation of what was required and progress to date across the city. It is also important to note that both men's surveys could have been converted into the other's format with time and effort. The manner in which surveying was deployed by the men who worked for the Paving Board therefore provides important insight into their technical training and background that is often missing from the commissioners' minute books. Throughout his time with the Paving Board, Brownrigg was effectively able to balance his new position alongside that as consultant surveyor and engineer to both the Grand and Royal Canal companies in addition to his private surveying practice until 1806.[401] By 1806, however, he had resigned from the Paving Board to focus his efforts on Ireland's growing canal system.[402]

About the time that Brownrigg was parting ways with the commissioners, a scathing investigative report was published into their activities since the reconstitution of the organisation in 1784. Like the previous complaints in the 1780s made about the Paving Board, this report was not without justification and was highly critical of the way in which the Paving Board operated, blaming them directly for 'the present ruinous state of the streets.'[403] This new investigation had been proposed in the British parliament that now directly ruled Ireland following the Act of

401 *Dublin Journal*, 21 Apr. 1789; Peter Clarke, *The Royal Canal* (Dublin, 1992), pp 27–35; John Brownrigg, 'Beresford Street' (1790) (NLI Longfield papers, MS 21F86(8)); John Brownrigg, 'Little Mary Street' (1804) (NLI Longfield papers, MS 21F86(30)); John Brownrigg, 'Holding on Charlemont Street' (1795) (NLI Longfield papers, MS 21f87(104)).
402 Delany, *The Grand Canal of Ireland*, p. 156.
403 LaTouche, et al., *Report of the commissioners*, p. 1.

Union (1801). Nicholas Vansittart (1766–1851), newly appointed chief secretary for Ireland under the administration of Prime Minister William Pitt the Younger (1759–1806), noted that the third Paving Board had

> either through mismanagement or from unfortunate circumstances, had got very considerably into debt, and the situation of the streets of Dublin was now absolutely disgraceful.[404]

Blaquiere (now a lord), bringing his considerable charm to bear before his peers 'rejoiced that the time for enquiry had arrived' and fully agreed that the situation on Dublin's streets was poor.[405] In defence of the institution he had created, he highlighted the increase in cost of materials used by the board, particularly the doubling of lamp oil costs since 1784, which had not been matched by a corresponding increase in taxation and that the principle part of the Paving Board's £84,000 debt was mostly inherited from the first two boards.[406] Fellow parliamentarian Dennis Browne (1763–1828) recounted a recent walk he had taken in Dublin at night where he, 'with some surprise, exclaimed that there was nothing but darkness, danger, and desolation' in regard to the lack of street lighting. Support for a full investigation was echoed by many of those present.[407]

Blaquiere and his fellow directors came in for particularly harsh treatment from the report committee and were noted for their poor attendance of meetings, a trait that had been *in situ* since the founding of the third Paving Board. Their absenteeism

> has necessarily weakened the authority and influence of the commissioners, their control over the subordinate officers, and their own sense of responsibility to the public, and by that means introduced a general laxity throughout the whole of the acting part of this establishment.[408]

This regular non-attendance from the Paving Board directors left a considerable power vacuum and lack of leadership for the entire organisation. The commissioners, operating as managers and advisors, were legally unable to make many of the executive-level decisions necessary for the development of the board, as this power

---

404 William Cobbett and John Wright, *Cobbett's parliamentary debates* (London, 1805), vol 5, p. 115.
405 Ibid.
406 Ibid.
407 Ibid.
408 LaTouche, et al., *Report of the commissioners*, p. 4.

lay in the hands of the directors. This was echoed by other commentators of the era who noted that the commissioners' ability to perform their duties was often greatly limited by their superiors:

> the material defect of [the Paving Board] is, that it separates the power from the responsibility, which should always be united. It is evident, that by this arrangement, the whole authority is lodged in the Directors, whilst the whole responsibility rests on the Commissioners, who have not the power of appointing, or displacing; of rewarding, or punishing, the officers under them; who are the only instruments through whom they can execute the complicated duties committed to their care: – If there be any failure in any part of the business, the blame is constantly imputed to them, while the Directors are placed above the reach of censure and calumny.[409]

Aside from such organisational problems and a noted degradation in the quality of materials used to pave Dublin's streets, primarily through the use of recycled paving slabs,[410] the investigators' main concern was rooted in a problem familiar to the Paving Board: financial and operational mismanagement. Dishonesty within the higher echelons trickled down through the organisation as there was a significant level of corruption from inspectors and collectors due to poor levels of supervision. Contractors were often left unpaid by the board and when such payments were eventually made they were highly infrequent. This left contractors in a difficult position as they could not maintain their services without a regular and steady income from the commissioners, yet risked being fined if such services were not fulfilled.[411] The Paving Board also had the added expenditure of having paid £5,000 for the construction of Sarah's Bridge (now renamed Islandbridge), a project it may not have been in the strongest financial state to undertake.[412] Subordinates hired by the Paving Board directors and commissioners were also scrutinised, including several elderly men who ran the board's main stone yard off Nassau Street and the highly suspicious hiring of John Blaquiere's personal butler as a collector in the fourth division, 'who never has been in Ireland since the date of his appointment'.[413]

---

409   J.R., *Letter from J-R- Esq., to his friend in England on the rise, progress and present state of the corporation for paving and lighting the city of Dublin* (Dublin, 1805), p. 10.
410   LaTouche, et al., *Report of the commissioners*, p. 5.
411   Ibid., p. 11.
412   Ibid., p. 22.
413   Evidence of Thomas King; ibid., p. 21.

The report's proposed recommendations must have been tough reading for Blaquiere, who had set out to reform the Paving Board after wrestling control of it away from Dublin Corporation back in 1784. The third Paving Board was simply inefficient and unmanageable in its present state. Despite noting the Paving Board's often 'energetic exercise of authority in enforcing the discharge of duty' the investigators found that

> the constitution of the present board ... is radically vicious, and ought to be totally changed, a system by which superintendence, control, and patronage, are all vested in one set of men, bound to no regular stated attendance.[414]

It seems as if the Paving Board was stuck in a destructive repetitive loop. Unable to remain functional in the light of such damning conclusions, the 1806 report marked the termination of the third, and the creation of yet another, Paving Board responsible for the capital's streets. All local jurisdictions related to paving, lighting and cleansing were to be abolished and control restored to a central paving authority 'armed with sufficient powers to correct the local abuses which abound'.[415] Much of the report's recommendations were put into place under new legislation;[416] yet despite such strong criticisms and calling for the body to be completely restructured, the quality of paving in the city did not come under significant fire. It seems that Blaquiere's Paving Board, despite its faults, did do some tasks correctly.

Another report, a duel and the fifth Paving Board

The daily work of maintaining Dublin's streets and dealing with its citizens carried on under the new regime brought about by the creation of the fourth Paving Board in 1807. One commentator at the time expressed the renewed hope that the fourth Paving Board had brought to the city now that they were 'freed from the embarrassments of their predecessors'.[417] Perhaps the most prominent change to the board's structure under this new governance was the removal of the role of director and a reduction in the number of commissioners to three. It was led from 1807 onwards by one of the chief investigators into Blaquiere's work, Major

---

414 Ibid., p. 29.
415 Ibid., p. 31.
416 47 Geo. III, c. 109 (1809).
417 Warburton, *History of the city of Dublin*, p. 448.

Alexander Taylor (1746–1828).[418] Taylor, a Scottish-born military engineer with extensive expertise in organising complex projects,[419] was cited as being one of the main causes for the improvements of Dublin's streets:

> [The Paving Board] under the direction of the enlightened judgement of the first commissioner, Major Taylor, whose firmness was necessary to resist much opposition and obloquy: our pavements, well bedded in gravel, have attained a durability before unknown; streets of the greatest resort are paved … [which] has facilitated the labour of the scavenger, which is regularly attended to.[420]

A notable event during this time was the Paving Board's assistance with Richard Lovell Edgeworth's *Essay on the construction of roads and carriages* (London, 1817). Edgeworth (1744–1817) was a politician, writer and inventor who had investigated methods of road construction and how carriages could be made to reduce the wear and tear of road surfaces.[421] As part of his studies, he had experimented with the use of different wood types for wheel axles as well as suspension springs for carriages, and in his findings to the Royal Dublin Society concluded 'Upon the whole, I beg leave to observe, that the chief thing to be attended to is, without any comparison, the goodness of the road'.[422] Edgeworth noted the work of Commissioner Taylor for his laying of gravel and allowing road traffic in Dublin to compact it for several months prior to the street being paved.[423] In retrospect this may not have been the most ideal method of foundation construction as surface water (see p. 116) and an unevenly compacted gravel layer could harm the road's long-term survivability, not to mention generating large quantities of dust during drier periods.[424] However, it was only through such experimentation by Edgeworth, Taylor and others across the world that road development was slowly improved during the early nineteenth century. Their work also showed that there was a distinct need to advance construction techniques, as the expansion of the industrial revolution and greater urbanisation demonstrated the distinct limitations of the existing transportation

---

418   James Moody, et al., *First report of the commissioners appointed to inquire into the municipal corporations in Ireland* (London, 1835), p. 78.
419   Andrews, *Plantation acres*, pp 105, 287–8, 350, 356–7.
420   Warburton, *History of the city of Dublin*, p. 449.
421   Richard Lovell Edgeworth, *An essay on the construction of roads and carriages* (London, 1817), p. 1.
422   Ibid., p. 170.
423   Ibid., p. 24.
424   Ibid., p. 449.

network. In his acknowledgments, Edgeworth thanked the Dublin Paving Board for their assistance with his research 'without which I could not have proceeded, without much delay and extraordinary expense'.[425]

Over time, older commissioners retired and new ones took their place. One of these, Major Thomas Newcomen Edgeworth (1778–1857), politician and relative to Richard Lovell Edgeworth, found himself at the centre of a major judicial trial in the 1820s when he was accused of borrowing £1,400 to purchase a controlling share in the Dublin newspaper, *The Evening Mail*. In the years leading up to this event, he had found himself in financially 'embarrassing circumstances' that required him to hand his estate to trustees to pay off a considerable debt.[426] At his trial, Edgeworth was referred to mockingly by the prosecution barrister as 'a member of that *popular* corporation, the commissioners for paving and lighting this city', indicating the lack of general public support the Paving Board had at the time.[427] Such comments were not without cause as, shortly before Edgeworth was taking the stand, yet another in a long litany of damaging reports had been published on the Paving Board's activities.

The 1826 report into the work of the Dublin Paving Board had been ordered by the chief secretary of Ireland, Henry Goulburn (1784–1856) and, much like the 1782, 1784 and 1806 reports, financial problems lay at its heart. A member of Dublin Corporation, Alderman Richard Smyth, had alerted authorities to the board and its treasurer, James Hendrick, of 'the most corrupt practices and grossest violations of duty, in applying the public money to their own purposes'.[428] Smyth, noted as having 'a most zealous desire to discharge his duty', claimed that the Paving Board's old habit of not paying contractors on time or sufficiently (as noted in 1806) was still ongoing, 'which of course was attended with the most mischievous consequences to the public interests'.[429] Attention was drawn to Chief Commissioner Taylor who had borrowed £800 from the Paving Board's accounts and was using the board's construction material for his own personal use.[430] Another dubious borrower was Edgeworth, who, in his dire monetary circumstances noted during his *Evening Mail* trial, had asked the Paving Board's treasurer for a loan simply because he was 'the first person he could apply to at the

---

425 Ibid., p. iii.
426 James Hall and William Deane Freeman, *Report of the commissioners for inquiring into the management and system of conducting the affairs of the Paving Board, Dublin* (London, 1826), p. 4.
427 Anon., *Report of a trial held in the court of exchequer* (Dublin, 1827), p. 6.
428 Hall and Freeman, *Report of the commissioners*, p. 3.
429 Ibid.
430 Ibid., p. 4.

time, and as a monied man'.[431] He had been noted by the investigators as having a positive role in reforming the Paving Board since his appointment; however, despite such praise his admittance of this loan had only been made after Smyth's accusations had come to light.

Aside from such findings, the main culprit in such fiscal irregularities was identified as being treasurer James Hendrick. He, along with his father who acted as assistant treasurer, had complete control of the Paving Board's finances and channelled public money to his own private purposes. The report's authors found

> [that] abuses have uniformly existed in his office, and every branch of the establishment connected with it, to a degree that cannot well be imagined, and that never could have taken place but for the grossest negligence.[432]

Hendrick had resigned in 1826 possibly because he knew the report would not be favourable for him. The corruption of its treasurer may also have encouraged the Paving Board's tax collectors to stray into illegality. These collectors were at the time found 'to have acted with the greatest negligence and partiality, and some of them most corruptly'.[433] Smyth, the self-appointed Paving Board reformer, had issued a memo to collectors on his appointment to take greater diligence with their duties, but this was subsequently retracted by the other commissioners, implying indirect support for off-the-book collections.[434]

As in 1806, the Paving Board had developed a reputation of being 'extremely irregular' in payments to contractors. Confidence in the commissioners to pay for goods and services was so poor that

> when advertisements were published by the board for the supply of any article, very few thought of sending in proposals, from the disappointments they knew they were liable to meet with, and the general impression that the commissioners could not be relied on in any engagement they entered into.

One source of such 'disappointments' was the haphazard manner in which the board recorded its minutes, often resorting to verbal commands. This is supported in the historical record, as accounts of meetings from the 1820s are of significantly

---

431   Ibid.
432   Ibid., p. 5.
433   Ibid., p. 8.
434   Ibid.

poorer quality than the regimented and highly detailed minute books during the period 1774–1806. Edgeworth had complained about this lack of minute-keeping on his appointment, but had been told that some of the issues discussed were highly confidential, thus lending weight to significant organisational mismanagement and the probability of funds being siphoned.[435]

Misallocation of resources could be seen throughout the body. Despite having ample funding for feed for the Paving Board's horses, numbering around thirty animals, the investigators found that they were greatly malnourished. They suspected that the person in charge of the creatures was stealing money meant for the horses' well-being, resulting in extreme animal cruelty.[436] Scavenging was also noted as being poorly monitored, as the commissioners were overpaying for hired carts, manure was being sold at lower prices than necessary and the depots were regularly being plundered.[437]

The investigators suggested that the office of treasurer should be abolished and that the Paving Board should consist of the commissioners, the office of accountant (formerly supervisor of works), the secretary and the pay-clerk, hoping that 'it is obvious that none but the most efficient persons should be employed, which is not the case at present'.[438] In a sign of the impact that the industrial revolution and technological developments were having on that era, the investigators also recommended that the Paving Board take note of the recent publication of John Loudon MacAdam (1756–1836), *Remarks on the present system of road making* (London, 1816) that described a new method of paving roads. MacAdam himself had noted that despite improvements in road construction, including his own methods,

> the reformation has not been more extensive and successful,
> [which] may be attributed to the error still persisted in by the
> Trustees [of turnpike roads in Britain], of continuing the services
> of persons as Road Surveyors, who are not only altogether
> ignorant of the business they profess, but full of prejudices in
> favour of their own erroneous practice.[439]

435   Ibid., p. 10.
436   Ibid., p. 11.
437   Ibid.
438   Ibid., p. 17.
439   John Loudon MacAdam, *Remarks on the present system of road making* (London, 1823),
          preface.

MacAdam's concise and logical approach of using a foundation of crushed rocks of uniform size coated with a cementing agent to keep out water revolutionised approaches to road construction. In the early twentieth century, his method was combined with a new tar-based road surfacing material resulting in what is known as tarmacadam, a familiar substance to all modern road users.

For former commissioner Edgeworth, the drama associated with his court trial and fallout from the 1826 investigation took an unusual twist. In September 1827, an article criticising one of the former paving commissioners and the manner in which he had behaved in office was published in the *Freeman's Journal*. Edgeworth, believing this article was directed at him, blamed the paper's owner Henry Grattan Jr (1787–1859) for allowing it to be published, stating that

> If I am forced into notoriety, the act is certainly not of my own seeking, my character having been falsely and slanderously attacked by a member of the Dublin press in his own paper.[440]

Demanding satisfaction and that his honour be restored, Edgeworth challenged Grattan to a duel with pistols. Unfortunately for the former Paving Board member, he was further frustrated when his opponent refused his challenge and continually failed to offer an apology for the offending article. The incident eventually petered out, but only after Edgeworth was further lambasted and ridiculed for his actions towards Grattan by other Dublin newspapers.[441]

440 *Saunders' Newsletter*, 15 Sept. 1827.
441 Joseph Hamilton, *The duelling handbook* (London, 1829), p. 92.

5.2   *Sackville Street, Dublin* by J. Newman (c.1840). Sackville Street (modern O'Connell Street) as it was during the time of the fifth Dublin Paving Board (courtesy of the National Library of Ireland © NLI).

With the problems with the fourth Paving Board finally exposed, Alderman Smyth, the great reformer of Taylor's fourth board, now found himself as chair of the new (fifth) Paving Board. Retaining the same small administrative set-up as the fourth Paving Board, he, along with fellow commissioners Colonel Morris and Hickman Kearney, went to work tackling many of the defects and managerial problems that had repeatedly surfaced over the past half century. Indeed, a report from a commission investigating the municipal corporations in Ireland in 1835 found the fifth Paving Board had managed to significantly increase collection of arrears to the sum of £8,000 'without an oppressive exercise of power, and principally by correcting the negligent, partial, and corrupt practices of the collectors'.[442] Minutes taken at board meetings had greatly developed in comparison to previous decades, documents related to business matters were being preserved and archived and the supervision of works had become very effective, but lack of revenue from taxation still remained a significant issue.[443]

End of the Dublin Paving Board

In the mid-nineteenth century a number of civic bodies, including the WSC, the PWC, and the Paving Board, were reviewed as part of a strategy to reform Dublin Corporation and the manner in which the city was run. This was part of an overall

442   Moody, *First report of the commissioners*, p. 78.
443   Ibid., p. 79.

effort to redevelop Ireland's urban councils under the Municipal Corporation Reform (Ireland) Act of 1840. The end of many of the city's eighteenth-century civic institutions was near. A team of investigators was employed to assess the Paving Board and its role in the city and found it a body 'which enjoys a greater amount of property and power of control than any other board in Dublin'.[444] Despite such great civic authority and the initial hopes of Alderman Smyth, the report determined that

> the present state of the streets of Dublin was very bad, that the mode of repairing and scavenging the streets, lanes and courts of the city was inefficient and expensive; that the mode of effecting contracts by the Board was improvident; that the Board was open to the charge of undue influence from the Government; and that the defects in their system of superintendence, and management of the affairs of the city entrusted to them, were such as to call for the step now proposed of transferring the powers and property vested in them to the a more responsible and trustworthy body.[445]

With the passing of An Act for the Improvement of the City of Dublin (1849), Dublin Corporation, sixty-five years after the College Green riot, fully retook control of 'the paving, lighting, cleansing, widening, and improving of the streets and thoroughfares'.[446] The Paving Board was at an end.

Given the often skewed relationship between the Paving Board, WSC and PWC – three totally separate organisations – it made strategic sense to incorporate these commissions under one governing body. The improvement act also allowed public funds to be controlled more efficiently from a centralised financial structure for the maintenance and development of Dublin's streets and avoid the multiple financial scandals that had rocked the various paving boards so publically since 1774.

The Paving Board had guided Dublin, at times inadequately, at others successfully, from a fractured and uneven network of self-focused urban parishes of the early eighteenth century to a structured, hierarchical and logical framework of city maintenance. This represented a substantial leap forward in civic administration and was perhaps its greatest achievement. What conclusions can be drawn from their work, and that of Thomas Owen, are discussed in the following section.

---

444   Henry Colles and Joseph James Byrne, *Report from the surveying officers on the Dublin Improvement Bill* (London, 1848), p. 263.
445   Ibid.
446   12 & 13 Vic., c. 97 (1849).

Conclusions

There are unusual parallels between the career of Thomas Owen as a surveyor and the formative years of the Dublin Paving Board. Both were capable of undertaking their assigned tasks with skill and were able to produce high-quality results, which were noted even by their critics. However, they both fell victim to fundamental problems – financial for the Paving Board, personal for Owen – that deeply impacted their respective roles.

Owen was a skilled measurer, architect and surveyor. The clear and precise plans he created during his work for the duke of Leinster demonstrate the product of a competent practitioner with a steady hand and an eye for detail. Being elected to the position of Paving Board surveyor in 1774 and 1782 over other high-quality candidates stands as a measure to his capabilities, as does his thirteen-year service in a central role. During that time, he demonstrated the importance that spatial measurement could have in organising large-scale engineering works. His measurements empowered decision makers and gave fascinating and unmatched detail into the state of Dublin's transport infrastructure during this era. The 1782 city-wide street survey he conducted was perhaps one of the most powerful pieces of evidence presented to parliament that led to the founding of the controversial third Paving Board. Yet, despite such positive aspects to his career, his frequent inability to complete work on time, as seen both during his building work at Frescati and on multiple occasions for the first three Paving Boards, coupled with questions about his honesty and occasional aggressiveness towards his superiors, hint at deeper issues not revealed by the historical record. The manner of his dismissal in 1787 was significant, as it revealed that while Owen was an important member of staff for the commissioners, he was not one of them. He was outside of the decision-making loop for the management of the organisation and was replaceable in the eyes of his employers. Being awarded alms on his dismissal, traditionally reserved for the more unfortunate members of society, may also indicate that he had no other form of income and had become over-reliant on the board. This was in stark contrast to other contemporary surveyors employed by similar organisations who successfully balanced both their official civic duties and private practises in tandem. Owen had dedicated himself to the Paving Board, which left him highly vulnerable to an unstable body rife with administrative, financial and management problems from its inception. Being surveyor to the Paving Board could never be a job for life.

The Paving Board played a fundamental role in bringing order to the world of late eighteenth-century Dublin's streets. While it would be easy to criticise its work in the light of the frequent damaging reports made against the board, it is important to remember that we look back at them from an era where the quality of street maintenance is very high. Modern civic maintenance operates to enforceable standards, public consultation and accountability that can trace their roots back to the work of the paving commissioners. It took a fragmented, out-dated and unbalanced system of quasi-medieval parochial control of street repairs and placed it under centralised governance. It applied a logical and systematic approach to improving Dublin's thoroughfares and sought to make the city an example of a safe, clean and beautiful urban environment, moving away from the inefficient system that had existed for centuries. Under its tenure, streets were well paved, cleaned on a regular basis and lit as best as possible, bringing increased levels of safety, hygiene and ease of communication. It helped improve a vital section of Dublin's civic infrastructure that would prove essential to helping the rapidly growing city function.

While their intentions were well placed, the board was profoundly flawed from its beginning, particularly when it came to finances. It lacked the initial revenue to carry out its mandate in the inappropriate timeframe set by the first board. If the commissioners of the original Paving Board had been patient, their funding from taxation may have been sufficient to support their work at a significantly slower pace. But by borrowing large sums of money in the mid-1770s to hurry along their projects, coupled with more minor issues such as diverting resources for political or personal favours and a lack of professional discipline among some of its officers, their labour became so financially twisted that they could never catch up with their monetary debts. Attempts by the second Paving Board were never going to succeed in repairing the damage done and the consequence of such mismanagement was the removal of this body from the elected governance of the city and the takeover by a small group of men with extensive powers over the populace.

The creation of the third Paving Board in 1784 proved a battleground for many different factions. At a civic level, it led to open discord between Dublin Corporation, responsible for running the city since the Middle Ages, and the Irish Parliament in a disagreement over who would control the capital's streets. Within parliament, it acted as yet another theatre for the increasingly passionate fight over the future role of Irish governance and the country's position within the British Empire, while at street level it provided a medium for disgruntled workers to voice their anger over the economic hardships they were forced to endure due to changes in government policy.

121

As the nineteenth century dawned, this group, without adequate supervision or accountability, was the subject of a damning report that ultimately led to the collapse of the third Paving Board and the creation of a new board which, in turn, fell victim to the same problems that had led to the collapse of its predecessors. Their 'exercise of authority' was caught in a disturbing loop of reorganisation, mismanagement, fraud and collapse. Dublin was growing rapidly and with an ever-increasing population; the 1849 Improvement Act brought the better funding and administration needed to meet Dublin's needs.

Through its work the Paving Board impacted the lives of Dublin's entire population, either through taxation, enforcement of rules or simply by their construction work in the warren of streets that made up the city's core. These impacts were, for the most part, quietly accepted by the populace of the city. However, when resistance was offered or the Paving Board's efforts entirely rejected, a glimpse can be gained into the often turbulent, lively and occasionally violent life of Dublin's Georgian-era streets and the multiple social groups that inhabited them. At times, the board responded with a heavy hand to such opposition, most notably in relation to assaults on its lamplighters on Capel Street, but for the most part, fines, summonses and the occasional short prison sentence issued by the commissioners ensured cooperation. Much like today, the city's neighbourhoods, whether they were slums, markets, upper class, industrial or artisan, each had distinct characteristics and unique qualities that were often shared by their residents. Familiar issues concerning public safety, traffic congestion, disagreements with neighbours and complaints over taxation add a human, and at times dramatic, element to what could potentially be a sterile examination of street paving, lighting and cleansing. It is through these stories, and the involvement of Paving Board employees, that the urban environment comes to life and we see that modern and eighteenth-century Dubliners have far more in common than may first appear.

Behind much of the work conducted by this body was Owen. He was a vital contributor to the Paving Board and thus to the development of the streets of Dublin. His daily supply of information in the form of accurate measurement and technical advice was the source on which the commissioners based some of their most important decisions. These decisions not only had significant financial implications but also, and more importantly, affected lives of Dubliners throughout the city. He quantified the city's streets and, despite the many issues that came from dealing with the vast array of residents, commissioners, contractors and directors, played his own small role in shaping late eighteenth-century Dublin. Ultimately, Thomas Owen was an imperfect man working for an imperfect organisation.

Appendix

The manner in which the various incarnations of the Dublin Paving Board were managed from 1774 to 1807 can perhaps be best seen in their respective administrative set-ups. Each embodiment was a reflection of the events and circumstances that led to its creation. The influence that Dublin Corporation had over the first Paving Board (1774–82) is demonstrated by its official distinction between aldermen and common council members, as per the corporation's hierarchy, and the compartmentalisation of each of its divisions into parochial committees. The second Paving Board (1782–4) was a makeshift solution to wider financial problems and thus lacked the distinct chain of command found in its predecessor's management. With the removal of Dublin Corporation from the daily workings of the body, the third Paving Board (1784–1807) was substantially more streamlined than those that had come before it. Meetings were attended on average by five or six commissioners who handled day-to-day decision making, while directors only attended infrequently. The 1806 report into the third Paving Board, and the subsequent foundation of the fourth (1807) and fifth (1827) embodiment of the organisation saw an even smaller number of commissioners required, bearing a similar executive committee as had existed when paving, lighting and cleansing had been under direct control of the lord mayor of Dublin.[447]

Paving Board members could resign and new ones elected in their place, so the list below only reflects the original committees for each board. It should be noted that both the second and third Paving Boards were also reliant on parochial committees during their tenure.

---

447   4 Geo. I, c. 2 [Ire.] (1717).

First Paving Board (1774)

Original commissioners, aldermen, common council and parochial board members per division:

First Division	Commissioner: James Agar Aldermen: Benjamin Geale, Henry Bevan, James Hamilton Commons: John Nugent, Robert Mahan, Ambrose Leet Parochial Committees: St Michan's: Revd Samuel Butler, W. Mc Muttrie, Richard Maxwell, Thomas Rotherham, Joseph Watson, William Gresson, William Ord, George Bryan St Paul's: Benjamin Garstin, Masuel Tindall, Henry Farrell, George Gibson
Second Division	Commissioner: Sydenham Singleton Esq. Aldermen: William Forbes, Joseph Lynham, Kilner Sweetenham Commons: Henry Howison, George Sutton, John Wilson Parochial Committees: St Thomas': Holt Warring Esq., Arthur Ormsby Esq., Plunket H. Talbot Esq., Joshua Parker, William Handock Esq., Arthur French Esq St Mary's: Henry Strong Esq., Richard Moncrieff, Henry Dobson, John Seaton, Gilbert Kilby
Third Division	Commissioner: Maj. Charles Vallancey Aldermen: Philip Crampton, Edward Sankey, Sir Thomas Blackhall Commons: John Hart Esq., Benjamin Ball Esq., George Darley Parochial Committees: St Mark's: John Marsden, Benj. Pemberton St Andrew's: William Adair, Robert Horne, John Binns Jr St Anne's: John Heydon, Timothy Turner, James Ormsby Esq. St Peter's: Thomas Classon, Samuel Collins, Richard Ginn
Forth Division	Commissioner: Travers Hartley Aldermen: Percival Hunt, George Wrightson, Thomas Emerson Commons: Isaac Boardman, John Roe, William Davis Parochial Committees: St John's: Christopher Hearn, John Graham St Michael's: Samuel Gamble, Peter Taylor St Bride's: Thomas Jones, George Wilson, James Shiel Esq. St Werburgh's: Edward Stanley, Thomas Dickson, Thomas Tudor St Nicholas Within: Benjamin Ward, William Bell

Fifth Division	Commissioner: Nicholas Morrison Esq.
	Aldermen: Henry Hart, Richard French, Francis Fetherston
	Commons: James Horan Esq., George Macquay Esq., Robert Hutton
	Parochial Committees:
	St Nicholas Without: Alexander Ross, Richard Fox, George Crain
	St Audeon's: Daniel Dickinson, George Sall, Sir Anthony King, James Jones Esq.
	St Catherine's: Mark Bloxham, Joseph Pike, Joshua Clibborne, Edward Geoghehan
	St James': Thomas Corles

Second Paving Board (1782)

Original commissioners per division:

First Division	Rt Hon. Lord Bective, Rt Hon. Lord Clifden, Rt Hon. Luke Gardiner, Warden Flood, Stephen Wybrants, Alderman Gale, William Bryan, William Lyster, John Leigh, Sherriff Dick
Second Division	Thomas Adderly, Edward Bell Swan, Hon. Richard Annesley, Sir Patrick King, John Godley, Robert Gamble, William Bury, William Handcock, William Deane, Lewis Laurent
Third Division	Thomas Kingsbury, Ambrose Smith, Nathanial Kavanagh, John Cornville, Morgan Crofton, Hon. Maj. John Butler, Thos. Thompson, Jonathan Ladevese, Alderman Crampton, Peter Maturin
Forth Division	Rt Hon. Lord Ranelagh, Travers Hartley, David LaTouche Jr, Thomas Ellis, Jonathan Patrickson, Richard Wallen, James Robinson, Michael Bally, Hamilton Stewart, Sherriff Campell
Fifth Division	Nicholas Morrison, Robert Thorp, John Hunt, William Lyster, Warden Flood, Hugh Boven, John Dillon, George Rochfort, Redmond Morres, Ephraim Hutchinson
Sixth Division	John Hatch, Sir Frederick Flood, Charles Domville, Samuel Forth, James Robinson, Thomas Tisdale, Stephen Dickson, John Wallis, George Curtland, Richard Maturin

Third Paving Board (1784)

Original commissioners and directors:

Directors	Thomas Kingsbury, Lord Ranelagh, Hon. Gen. Luttrell, John Leigh, Rt Hon. Lord Clifden, Rt Hon. Sir John Blaquiere
Commissioners	James Ormsby, William Lightburn, William Alexander, Hugh Henry Mitchell, Capt. John Hall

Fourth Paving Board (1807)

Commissioners	Major Alexander Taylor, Alderman Henry Hutton, Alderman Frederick Darley

Fifth Paving Board (1827)

Commissioners	Alderman Richard Smyth, Colonel George Morris, Hickman Kearney Esq.

Bibliography

Manuscript primary sources

Dublin City Archives (DCA)
Dublin city surveyors' book of maps (1695–1827).
Dublin Paving Board Minute Books, vols 1–36 (1774–1801).

Irish Architectural Archive (IAA)
McParland, Edward, files, acc/2008/44.

Marsh's Library (ML)
Anon., Dublin church wardens agreement concerning the
lighting and cleaning of streets (1725) MS 1725.

National Library of Ireland (NLI)
Longfield, John, 'Maps and plans of estates, Dublin' (1724–1847), MS 21F86–90.

Acts of British and Irish parliaments

9 Will. III, c. 17 [Ire.] (1697).
4 Geo. I, c. 2 [Ire.] (1717).
4 Geo. I, c. 9 ss 6–11 [Ire.] (1717).
6 Geo. I, c. 15 [Ire.] (1719).
3 Geo. II, c. 13 [Ire.] (1725).
31 Geo. II, c.19 [Ire.] (1757).
33 Geo. II, c. 18 [Ire.] (1759).
13 & 14 Geo. III, c. 34 [Ire.] (1774).
15 & 16 Geo. III, c. 20 [Ire.] (1775).
21 & 22 Geo. III, c. 60 [Ire.] (1782).
25 Geo. III, c. 108 [Ire.] (1786).
26 Geo. III, c. 24 [Ire.] (1786).
26 Geo. III, c. 61 [Ire.] (1786).
47 Geo. III, c. 109 (1809).
12 & 13 Vic., c. 97 (1849).

Printed primary sources

Anon., *A letter to the linen-manufacturers of Ireland* (Dublin, 1784).

Anon., *Observations on the paving acts: reports, execution of works, &c., addressed to those whom it may concern* (Dublin, 1782).

Anon., *The lamplighter's poem* (London, c.1794).

Anon., *The lamplighter's poem* (London, c.1760).

Anon., *Report of a trial held in the court of exchequer* (Dublin, 1827).

Brooking, Charles, *A map of the city and suburbs of Dublin* (London, 1728).

Callan, Peter, *A dissertation on the practice of land surveying in Ireland; and an essay towards a general regulation therein* (Drogheda, 1758).

Cobbett, William and John Wright, *Cobbett's parliamentary debates* (London, 1805).

Colles, Henry and Joseph James Byrne, *Report from the surveying officers on the Dublin Improvement Bill* (London, 1848).

Curry, William, *The picture of Dublin: or, stranger's guide to the Irish metropolis* (Dublin, 1835).

Edgeworth, Richard Lovell, *An essay on the construction of roads and carriages* (London, 1817).

Ferrar, John, *A view of ancient and modern Dublin, with its improvements to the year 1796* (Dublin, 1796).

Gibson, Robert, *A treatise of practical surveying: which is demonstrated from its first principles* (Dublin, 1753).

Grey, John, *The art of land-measuring explained* (London, 1757).

Hall, James and William Deane Freeman, *Report of the commissioners for inquiring into the management and system of conducting the affairs of the Paving Board, Dublin* (London, 1826).

Hamilton, Joseph, *The duelling handbook* (London, 1829).

Hammond, John, *The practical surveyor: containing the most approved methods for the surveying of lands and waters ...* (London, 1765).

Hawney, William, *The complete measurer; or, the whole art of measuring* (London, 1730).

Hodgson, P. Levi, *The modern measurer, particularly adapted to timber and building, according to the present standard of the kingdom of Ireland* (Dublin, 1793).

LaTouche, John, et al., *Report of the commissioners appointed to enquire into the conduct and management of the corporation for paving, cleansing and lighting the streets of Dublin* (Dublin, 1806).

Leybourn, William, *The works of Edmund Günter: containing the description and use of his sector, cross-staff, bow, quadrant, and other instruments ...* (London, 1662).

MacAdam, John Loudon, *Remarks on the present system of road making* (London, 1823).

Martindale, Adam, *The country survey book* (London, 1702).

Moody, James, et al., *First report of the commissioners appointed to inquire into the municipal corporations in Ireland* (London, 1835).

Moody, T.W., R.B. McDowell and C.J. Woods (eds), *The writings of Theobald Wolfe Tone, 1763–98*, 2 vols (Oxford, 2009).

Nemo, John, *A brief record of the female orphan house* (Dublin, 1893).

Noble, Benjamin, *Geodesia Hibernica* (Dublin, 1768).

Pool, Robert and John Cash, *Views of the most remarkable public buildings, monuments and other edifices in the city of Dublin* (Dublin, 1780).

J.R., *Letter from J-R- Esq., to his friend in England on the rise, progress and present state of the corporation for paving and lighting the city of Dublin* (Dublin, 1805).

Richardson, George, *Iconology; or, a collection of emblematical figures, moral and instructive* (London, 1779).

Rocque, John, *An exact survey of the city and suburbs of Dublin* (Dublin, 1756).

Swift, Jonathan, *A description of a city shower* (London, 1710).

Waddington, J., *A description of instruments used by surveyors: ... the practical method of finding the altitudes and distances of terrestrial objects. Land surveying, ... levelling, and the method of dividing land* (London, 1773).

Warburton, John, *History of the city of Dublin* (London, 1818).

Wilson, Peter, *Wilsons' Dublin directory* (Dublin, 1783–1800).

Wyld, Samuel, *The practical surveyor* (London, 1725).

Newspapers

Dublin Chronicle (1788).

Dublin Evening Post (1782–4).

Dublin Gazette (1760).

Dublin Journal (1749–87).

Freeman's Journal (1774–82).

Leinster Journal (1774).

Saunders' Newsletter (1827).

The Penny Magazine (1837).

Universal Advertiser (1753).

Volunteers Journal (1784).

Secondary sources

Andrews, J. H., *Plantation acres* (Omagh, 1985).

Bendall, Sarah, *Dictionary of land surveyors and local map makers of Great Britain and Ireland, 1530–1850*, 2 vols (London, 1997).

Clark, Mary, *The book of maps of the Dublin city surveyors, 1695–1827* (Dublin, 1983).

Clarke, Peter, *The Royal Canal* (Dublin, 1992).

Cokayne, George Edward (ed.), *The complete baronetage*, 5 vols (London, 1900).

Colley, Mary, 'A list of architects, builders, surveyors, measurers and engineers extracted from Wilson's Dublin directories, 1760–1837', *IGSB*, 34 (1991), 7–68.

Craig, Maurice, *Dublin 1660–1860* (Dublin, 2006).

Delany, Ruth, *The Grand Canal of Ireland* (Dublin, 1995).

Fitzgerald, Brian (ed.), *Correspondence of Emily, duchess of Leinster III* (Dublin, 1957).

Frock, Linda, *Building capitalism* (London, 1991).

Gilbert, J.T. (ed.), *Calendar of ancient records of Dublin in the possession of the municipal corporation*, 19 vols (Dublin, 1889–1944).

Green, James, *Mathew Carey* (Philadelphia, 1985).

Griffen, David & Pegum, Caroline, *Leinster House 1744–2000, an architectural history* (IAA, 2000).

Herlihy, Jim, *The Dublin metropolitan police* (Dublin, 2001).

Kelly, James, *The Liberty and Ormond boys* (Dublin, 2005).

McBride, Ian, *Eighteenth-century Ireland* (Dublin, 2009).

McGuire, James and James Quinn (eds), *The dictionary of Irish biography*, 9 vols (Cambridge, 2009).

McManus, Ruth & Lisa Marie Griffith (eds), *Leaders of the city* (Dublin, 2013).

Ó Cionnaith, Finnian, *Mapping, measurement and metropolis: how land surveyors shaped eighteenth-century Dublin* (Dublin, 2012).

Refausé, Raymond (ed.), *Register of the parish of St. Thomas, Dublin 1750-1791* (RCB, 1994).

Sheridan, Edel, 'Designing the capital city' in Anngret Simms and Joseph Brady (eds), *Dublin through space and time* (Dublin, 2001), pp 66–135.

Index

House of Commons. *see*
    Irish parliament
Howard, Peter, 90
Howison, Henry, 124
Hunt, John, 125
Hunt, Percival, 124
Hutchinson, Ephraim, 125
Hutton, Henry, 126
Hutton, Robert, 125

Iconology, 16
industrial revolution, 113, 116
industry, 2, 34, 45, 46, 80.
    see also surveying
inspectors. *see* lighting inspectors;
    nuisance inspectors
instruments. *see under* surveying
Irish parliament, 2, 3, 4, 5, 7, 8, 10, 49,
    64–65, *84*, 121
    and College Green paving riot
    (1784), 83–88
    legislative independence and reform,
    81, 82
    and Paving Boards, 64, 65–67,
    69–70, 74, 76. *see also* legislation
Irish Volunteers, 81
Islandbridge, 111

Jackson, Thomas, 62
Johnston, George, 60
Johnston, William, 60
Jones, James, 125
Jones, Thomas, 124
jurisdiction, 48

Kavanagh, Nathanial, 125
Kearney, Hickman, 118, 126
Kelly, James, 49
Kelner, John, 36
Kendrick, Roger, 23

Kennedy, William, 60n
Kenny, Nicholas, *84*
Kilby, Gilbert, 124
King, Sir Anthony, 125
King, John Price, 58
King, Sir Patrick, 125
Kingsbury, Thomas, 125, 126
Kirwan Street, 60

La Touche, David Jr, 7n, 34, 36, 125
Ladevese, Jonathan, 125
lamp tax, 92–94, 98
lamplighters, 90, *91*, 91–92, 94, *95*, 98.
    see also lighting of streets
    assaults on, 94–100, 122
    criminal acts, 96
Lamplighter's poem, The,
    92, 94–95, *95*, 99
land surveyors. *see* surveyors
Laurent, Lewis, 125
Leet, Ambrose, 124
legislation, 8, 9, 22–23, 61, 62,
    104, 112, 119. *see also* Dublin
    Improvement Act (1849)
    Paving Acts, 7, 10, 67, 69–70,
    83–88, 93
    protest against Blaquiere's
    bill (1784), 83–88
Leigh, John, 88, 125, 126
Leinster, duchess of. *see*
    FitzGerald, Lady Emily
Leinster, duke of (James
    FitzGerald), 109, 120
Leinster House, Kildare
    Street, 17, 18, *20*
Lennox, Emily. *see* FitzGerald,
    Lady Emily
Lennox, Louisa. *see* Conolly,
    Lady Louisa
Liberties, 2, 10, 92–93